THE LAST CHOICE

**Recent Titles in
Contributions in Philosophy**

THE LAST CHOICE

Preemptive Suicide in Advanced Age

C. G. Prado

CONTRIBUTIONS IN PHILOSOPHY, NUMBER 41

GREENWOOD PRESS
New York • Westport, Connecticut • London

Library of Congress Cataloging-in-Publication Data

Prado, C. G.
   The last choice : preemptive suicide in advanced age / C. G. Prado.
      p.   cm.—(Contributions in philosophy, ISSN 0084–926X ; no.
41)
   Includes bibliographical references.
   ISBN 0–313–27301–4 (lib. bdg. : alk. paper)
   1. Aged—Suicidal behavior. 2. Suicide—Moral and ethical
aspects. 3. Euthanasia—Moral and ethical aspects. I. Title.
II. Series.
HV6545.2.P7   1990
362.2'8'0846—dc20   89–25735

British Library Cataloguing in Publication Data is available.

Library of Congress Catalog Card Number: 89–25735
ISBN: 0–313–27301–4
ISSN: 0084–926X

First published in 1990

Greenwood Press, 88 Post Road West, Westport, CT   06881
An imprint of Greenwood Publishing Group, Inc.

Printed in the United States of America

∞™

The paper used in this book complies with the
Permanent Paper Standard issued by the National
Information Standards Organization (Z39.48–1984).

10 9 8 7 6 5 4 3 2 1

For Nancy
In Memoriam

Kleombrotos . . .
Leaped down to Hades from a high wall:
Driven by no evil
To suicide,
But only that he had read
Plato's . . . mighty treatise on the Soul.

Kallimachos, 305 B.C.

CONTENTS

INTRODUCTION: COHERENCE, PREFERENCE, AND DEATH

> Free to die and free in death, able to say a holy No when
> the time for Yes has passed . . .
>
> Nietzsche, *Zarathustra*

My aim in this book is basically to recapture for our time something of the pre-Christian view of suicide as sometimes the wisest course of action, and as not necessarily an irrational or dishonorable act. In particular I want to recapture that attitude toward suicide in advanced age.

The project will seem at once timely and unnecessary: timely because of our aging population and the recent significant rise in elderly suicides, and unnecessary because of a "growing acceptance of the concept of 'rational suicide' " (Tolchin, 1989). But this book is necessary because the ways in which suicide is thought "rational" are too often confused and relativistic; because cultural attitudes remain largely obstructive; and because the acceptance and practice of suicide is still mainly restricted to suicide as release from unendurable pain. What follows is devoted to showing how an aging individual may rationally and advisedly choose to commit what I call "preemptive suicide," and which I distinguish from suicide forced by desperation, confusion, or compulsion. Preemptive suicide is the arguably rational way of avoiding not actual, intolerable conditions, but foreseen demeaning decline. My hope is partly to revitalize an old understanding of suicide, and partly to change our present understanding of suicide. The objective is to enable consideration of suicide as an *elective* choice, rather than as always the most drastic of responses.

The Central Questions

The issue most pivotal to my project is whether suicide can be rational—as opposed to being *a*rational because pathological, or *ir*rational because the result of fatal misconception. This is a complex issue because "rational" has several different senses in this application, and to claim that suicide is rational is to say several different things about the taking of one's own life. The question at the core of whether suicide can be rational is if it is coherent *to prefer to die*, or whether there is some conceptual inconsistency in an existing entity wanting cessation of existence. The purely logical question is if it is somehow contradictory to exist and prefer not to exist, as it would be contradictory to—at the same time—prefer to exist and prefer not to exist. However, this logical question is not here of major interest because a contradiction arises only if we allow matters-of-fact and desires to be contradictories, or allow two desires to contradict one another as their propositional statements may do. Considerably more important are two less formal aspects of the coherency question: first, whether we are capable of fully *understanding* the consequences of suicidal action to be personal annihilation, and so are capable of intentionally preferring and choosing imminent death over the palpable continuation of life; second, whether understanding carries over to *enactment*: whether we are capable of enacting our preference to die without self-deception. And the first aspect of the coherency question raises a subordinate issue important enough to require mention even at this early stage, namely, what one can intelligibly intend to *achieve* in choosing to die. For the preference to die to be coherent, we must be able to say how death can be a desirable objective, and how an agent can consider and undertake a course of action which has her own annihilation as its end.

Understanding the consequences of suicide and what suicide achieves cannot be a matter of "mere" understanding on the part of the agent. Conception and imagination obviously differ, and we cannot require that someone actually be able to *imagine* being dead as the result of considered action. But the enormity and irrevocable nature of suicide require more than mere conceivability or literal understanding of death to serve as the key deliberative element in its consideration. It is unsatisfactory to answer the question whether a potential suicidist understands what she is contemplating by saying that she understands what the word "death" means. The "more" required is a depth of understanding that is hard to articulate precisely but seems intuitively clear and has been described as "vivid awareness of . . . consequences" in deliberation (Harman, 1986: 2). What we find most problematic about the consideration of suicide is whether there can be "vivid awareness" of the consequences of the considered act, for we are not sure what it could be to have vivid awareness of one's own annihilation as an end to action. Some—particularly Freudians—think that at the unconscious level no one can really accept the reality of personal annihilation, so no one can fully understand the consequences of committing suicide. If the Freudians are right, then it is difficult to see the force of saying that someone's preference for death could be coherent and her decision to die could be well-reasoned. We might conclude that even when abstract criteria for coherence and sound deliberation are satisfied, taking one's own life still falls short of being rational because, in the event, the preference for death is always distorted by some overriding self-deceptive factor which systematically obscures that death is personal annihilation. If there is psychological preclusion of adequate understanding of death, if understanding does not carry over into suicidal action, then preferring to die cannot be coherent, because in every instance the preference would actually be for something *other* than death. That is, though it may be possible to reach a point where one coherently prefers to die, and chooses to die for good reason, it may not be possible to enact the preference and decision without some measure of self-deception. The parallel here is to the way physiology precludes our killing ourselves by simply holding our breath. There may well be reflexive psychological factors, just as there are reflexive physiological ones, which override cognitive and intentional ones in suicidal action. (I use "intentional" in Franz Brentano's "directedness-of-consciousness" sense; see Edwards, 1967: 201–4.) If so, then regardless of how rational the deliberative lead-up to suicide might be, no actual suicide could be a rational act because self-deceptive elements would be operant in the enactment of even the best-reasoned suicidal decision. The matter of what one intends or hopes to gain in committing suicide is here obviously relevant. Personal annihilation, the cessation of one's own existence, is at least intuitively a very strange object of intention. This is evident in that annihilation as an objective is invariably described in comparative terms—that is, in terms of annihilation being better than some alternative. For there to be adequate understanding that self-inflicted death is self-caused personal annihilation, it must be possible to give an account of what the potential suicidist intends to achieve in ceasing to exist, and also how the notion of achievement applies to a subject whose existence ends with the act in question. However, we must be careful to differentiate between the relevant difficulties just mentioned and empirical-theoretical preclusions of rational suicide. As we will see in Chapter 3, empirical claims—such as a putative psychological inability to believe one will cease to exist—are subordinate to the coherency and intentional-objective aspects of the question whether suicide can be rational. In spite of negative theoretical claims about our psychological capabilities regarding suicide, if we can say how it is coherent to prefer to die, and how doing so can have an intelligible objective, cases of fully rational suicide must be considered as *possible*.

Summing up this preliminary sorting of issues, to ask if suicide is rational is to ask a number of questions, chief among them being whether it is coherent to prefer and choose to die, and what it is one can intend to achieve in dying; and whether, given the coherency of preferring to die, one can act on the preference in a fully knowing and well-reasoned manner. Whatever else may be said about suicide, it cannot be rational if we cannot understand that what we consider, prefer, and intend is personal annihilation, or if we cannot knowingly and intentionally act to achieve personal annihilation without somehow thinking it less than cessation of existence.

A Different Emphasis

My reason for undertaking the somber project of showing suicide to be sometimes rational and advisable arises from my work on aging (Prado, 1983, 1986, 1988; see also McKee, 1988). I believe that elective death in advanced age must be recognized as a sensible alternative to demeaning deterioration and stultifying dependency. My belief is supported by good evidence that most of the recent increase in elderly suicides is due to growing unwillingness by the old to endure the very mixed benefits of medically and technologically lengthened life spans (Tolchin, 1989; McIntosh, 1986). However, mere recognition of suicide as a sensible option would be insufficient, even if elective death in advanced age were widely acknowledged as a rational option. Advanced age itself raises questions about our reasoning and priorities—as I outline in Chapter 2. Dependence on the advice and judgment of others then becomes crucial for testing the validity of deliberations and decisions about choosing to die. But even if suicide were generally accepted as sometimes rational, at present still-dominant negative attitudes toward suicide would preclude effective help in the consideration of elective death. It is therefore necessary not only to gain concession of the rationality of suicide, but to change prevalent attitudes enough for potential suicidists to receive supportive and productive counseling. It is also necessary that there be medical willingness to provide painless ways to end life. The option of rational preemptive suicide in advanced age must be made a *practical* reality. Suicide must both be recognized as a rational option in old age, and its consideration—if not its actual enactment—facilitated by willing help for the potential suicidist. It cannot be left to small and usually marginally financed organizations, such as the Hemlock Society, to help the old who choose to die. Moreover, given the advanced age of the potential suicidist, and hence the likelihood of intimate custodial involvement in her life by family members and health-care practitioners, attitudes must be changed to prevent well-intentioned but essentially patronizing obstruction of the potential suicidist's deliberation and action.

My project differs from recent numerous treatments of euthanasia, euthanatic suicide, and suicide, in a crucial way: it does not focus on so-called "surcease" suicide or self-inflicted death as escape from pressing and desperate circumstances such as terminal illness (Kushner, 1989; DeSpelder and Strickland, 1987: 413). Suicide forced by life's becoming literally unbearable—suicide as *release*—has always been and remains an option, regardless of how despised or counseled against it may be, or, for that matter, how problematic its rationality. What we have lost is not the option of dying by our own hand when we are all but dead or have only unthinkable alternatives, but rather the option of suicide as a viable *preemptive* measure. Christian values have deprived us of the autonomy to "will at the right time to die" (Nietzsche, 1967: 484) when that decision is made on the basis of what we believe and expect, rather than on the basis of what has already happened to us. We must reclaim the right to decide that we have lived long enough, to decide that by living longer we risk the value of what we have achieved in our lives merely for the sake of sheer survival. I speak here of loss because it is very difficult, in our culture, to consider the possibility of deliberately ending our own lives unless we are thought to have overwhelmingly compelling reasons of an actively threatening sort. It is not simply a matter of moral or legal disagreement about the rightness of suicide. The attitudes necessary for discussion and consideration of *preemptive* suicide simply are not in place. Diagnoses of terminal cancer or Alzheimer's disease may be accepted as properly raising the question of suicide, but few contemporaries see suicide as possibly an elective option as opposed to always a forced choice. Suicide generally is not taken as a properly considerable course of action if that consideration is prompted only by reflective judgment, made prior to serious pressures, that it may be time to trade whatever life is left for the privilege of ending our lives on our own terms. Nor do we have to go back to pagan Greeks and Romans to find acceptance of suicide as an elective option. David Hume considered "that a man of sixty-five, by dying, cuts off only a few years of infirmities" (Hume, 1963a: 615). At the end of his life, when he knew he was dying, Hume thought that even the enjoyment of the literary fame he had so long sought would add only short-lived pleasure to a life from which he felt distanced and which he was ready to quit. Hume, in spite of his sensible views on suicide, did not take his own life, but most likely because he was saved the need to do so by being very fortunate in the manner of his terminal illness and death. Once his illness was diagnosed, he tells us he "reckon[ed] upon a speedy dissolution." And his death was enviable in that he was still able, at the very end, to banter with the likes of James Boswell (Hume, 1963a: 615; Boswell, 1947). But the sad fact is that, given our biological nature, few of us can count on an easy death. Much more often death comes cruelly, its onset destroying us as persons before death itself destroys us as beings. It is the possibility of trading good time left for the certainty of avoiding a bad death that our present culture largely denies us. Hume anticipated Nietzsche's admonition that everyone "must . . . practice the difficult art of leaving at the right time" (Nietzsche, 1954: 184), but few in our era can act on that admonition, thinking as they mostly do, that suicide is always wrong except when virtually inescapable. The Christian view is that our lives simply are not ours to take. From the early Church Fathers to the contemporary minister or parish priest, suicide is damned as a presumptuous and illegitimate disposition of a God-created and so God-owned life. Duties to one's community and family are quickly brought in to bolster the prohibition, but the root of the prohibition, and of the attitudes it generates, is the belief that our lives are not our own.

Aside from proposing suicide as an option in less than desperate circumstances, another way my project differs from more standard treatments of suicide is that unlike most, it does not center on ethical questions. First, I believe that ethical questions about elective death cannot be resolved in the abstract. I do not believe that there are universal and ahistorical standards available to us which determine the ethical rightness or wrongness of suicide independently of time, place, and circumstances. Second, I think there is a deep confusion in much ethical thinking about suicide, given that it incorporates two incompatible ideas, namely, that suicide is wrong, and that suicide is never fully rational. Given these two ideas, it would seem that the only sound ethical indictment of suicide would focus on the wrongness of *considering* it. That wrongness would be due to the danger that mere consideration of suicide might prompt its arational or irrational commission. The point here is that if suicide is never rational, it cannot itself be a fully responsible and so culpable act, hence not an act that can be meaningfully prohibited as ethically wrong. Ethics, then, should focus only the consideration of suicide. Yet suicide is invariably condemned as wrong as an act. But aside from abstract ethical considerations, clearly particular ethical beliefs will figure prominently in a potential suicidist's deliberations, and just as clearly some ethical values, and certainly most religious ones, will preclude the possibility of suicide for many. However, I am not concerned to argue against specific ethical or religious views. The issue I am addressing is whether suicide can even pose an ethical issue, or must always fail to do so because it is never rational. My thesis that suicide can be rational is quite compatible with any number of ethical systems prohibiting suicide because of alleged wrongness. Any system that judges suicide to be *wrong* must allow that cases of suicide, in being culpable, are knowing and deliberate, and so possibly rational though contrary to the code in question. What I want to defeat is the idea that suicide is *never* a rational act unless forced by the most extreme circumstance. This latter position is not an ethical stand against suicide, though it is dubiously used to support ethical prohibition of it. This position classifies suicide as always an essentially irresponsible act, because always at least partly a consequence of confusion or compulsion. The contrary position is not that all instances of suicide are rational, but that some suicidists are fully responsible for their acts and so some instances of suicide may be rational. It is a further matter to establish that a given set of ethical values does or does not condone rational suicide and to argue for either view. If suicide is never rational, ethical questions about it, and ethical prohibitions against it, are ultimately pointless. And ethical defenses of suicide would be equally pointless.

As suggested above, what prompts my project is that as our population ages, in the sense that the proportion of people over sixty-five increases, and as medical and nutritional sciences keep even more people alive whose survival would otherwise be highly problematic, it becomes pressing to see that it is within our power to rationally and responsibly judge at some point that we have lived long enough, and that further survival would be only for its own sake. At present, recognition that life should sometimes be given up is too limited to cases where life is preserved at great cost under medical conditions that would be fatal except for the intervention of modern technology. So-called "living wills," testaments that enjoin medical practitioners not to be excessive in their efforts to keep the testator alive, are an indication that more people are beginning to think twice about life being worth preserving at all costs. And as noted, there is significant evidence that as more people become aware of the nature of technological extension of life, and of the personal and economic costs involved, the quality of life thus gained increases in importance and greater resistance is shown to reliance on artificial techniques and devices (Tolchin, 1989; Shipp, 1988; note also recent media coverage such as a *60 Minutes* segment on elderly suicides, CBS, Nov. 19, 1989). But it is not only hopelessly incapacitated persons kept alive on respirators, or individuals only weeks away from an inevitable and agonizing death, who might better die sooner. We should all be able to choose to end our lives before deteriorating to a point where meaningless survival is all we have left. This means that our culture must come to recognize the legitimacy of some cases of suicide, that people must learn to respect, and not only deplore, someone's choice to die, and that potential suicidists must not be burdened with the weight of others' expectations and disapproval. A loved one's emotional pressure can be as imprisoning to someone wanting to die as any doctor's ill-advised and overly diligent efforts to keep them alive.

My argument for preemptive suicide's rationality is intended to show that people are capable of freely choosing to die before their minds and bodies finally betray them, and that the option to end our lives should be made more culturally acceptable and stripped of present connotations of cowardice and immorality. The result of the argument's success would be the enhancement of lives lived to their ends *by choice*. The argument seeks to foster emulation of Nietzsche, who wanted a "free death" of his own choosing and did not want to be like the ropemakers who "drag out their threads and always walk backwards" (Nietzsche, 1954: 184).

Clarification of Terms

Assuming the foregoing sections have succeeded in sketching the nature of the discussion to follow, it is now necessary to clarify in a preliminary way the key terms I use in this and subsequent chapters. The sense of rational in my phrase "rational preemptive suicide" has first to do with the coherency of preferring to die. Preemptive suicide must be rational in the sense that the preference to die, the decision to enact that preference, and the deliberation leading to that decision, all must be about something which can be fully comprehended, and so deliberated about and opted for in a knowing and adequately reflective way. If an individual prefers to die rather than risk living under abhorrent conditions, that preference is coherent only if she fully understands what it is to die, namely, that it is to utterly cease to exist. If the individual's preference is actually for quitting life as a way of entering what she knowingly or self-deceptively construes as a state of continued awareness in some other mode, her preference to die would not be coherent. The reason is that her preference would not really be a preference for death but for a different sort of existence. Minimally, then, the coherency of preferring death to life requires full appreciation that death is the cessation of existence. Suicide considered and committed in the grip of secular or religious belief in an afterlife is not rational because of the presence of incoherency (this is an admittedly arguable point and I shall return to it in Chapter 3). I might now offer a first approximation of how preemptive suicide may be rational: given full understanding of precisely what is considered and chosen, rational suicide would also include the following more familiar considerations—first, the deliberation leading to preemptive suicide must be free of inconsistency; second, the course of action must be the most utile, given operant values, objectives, and circumstances; and third, the pondering and choosing must be consistent in the different sense that, given the same circumstances and the same evaluation of relevant factors, the objective and chosen course of action would be the same in diverse cases.

The foregoing are all complex points, and more will be said about each later, but there is another and likely contentious point to be made here about the rationality of suicide. As I am using the term "rational," the rationality of preemptive suicide cannot be relativistically conceived. I can clarify what I mean with a typical definition of rational suicide. The *Dictionary of Modern Thought* assures us that someone's suicide "may be regarded as rational, if he prefers death to any other possible future." But the *Dictionary* goes on to say that "society may regard his death as an undesirable aim, in which case society would not regard the act of suicide as rational" (Bullock et al., 1988: 721). I do not accept this too relativistic sense of "rational" in spite of the fact that, as I will explain, I reject ahistorical conceptions of rationality. The foregoing use allows too facile a distinction between what is deemed rational by an individual and by a group or society at large. The way that I am using rational requires that there be a critical universality of judgment about suicide, and that suicide is not regarded as rational only in a sense in which suicide's rationality follows on its consistency with particular personal or group values. Unfortunately, as suggested above, much discussion about the growing acceptance of suicide turns on just this relativistic sense of rational. Essentially, the claimed acceptance is only higher tolerance of individual suicidal judgments, not acknowledgement of the rational justification of those judgments. When we are told that "the concept of rational suicide is gaining credence" (Tolchin, 1989), the operant sense of rational is too closely tied to individual and group values to serve productively and *reliably* in either suicidal deliberation or assessment of it—which is one reason for this book. Consider that regardless of the suicidist's or her peers' view of the matter, suicide would never be rational if, as some charge and we will consider in Chapter 3, there can be no intelligible contrast drawn in deliberating whether death is preferable to continued life. Again, as indicated, suicide would never be rational if the intention to die always involves some misconception about continued awareness after death. (As we will also see in Chapter 3, the most common element in pathological cases of suicide is expectation of posthumous satisfaction.) Moreover, suicide would never be rational if, as also indicated, every case of suicide is one of self-deceptive or compulsive psychological factors finally outweighing reasoned ones. Nonetheless, the relativistic sense of rational does capture something important. Regardless of how basic the matter, the rationality of suicide cannot be addressed purely in terms of the conceptual coherency of the preference to die. The reason is that "rational" has still more senses than those mentioned when applied to suicide. Aside from the sense at work in the question about the coherency of the preference to die, and the somewhat more extended senses having to do with utility and with deliberative and behavioral consistency, there definitely is a sense of "rational" having to do with the consistency of suicide with the suicidist's values. This is the sense which becomes relativistic when it is mistakenly thought to be exhaustive and when agent-values are too simplistically contrasted with group values. But this sense not only has legitimate application to whether an agent's values are better served by her death than by her continued existence, her suicide *must* be consistent with her values to be rational. This requirement may even challenge the values themselves. For example, an individual who endorses certain ethical or religious values simply cannot entertain suicide as an option. In some circumstances this preclusion will force reassessment of the values and raise questions about their justification. The values may consequently be rejected as not justifiable and so not serve as a bar to preemptive suicide. And the moment values are open to question, we realize that they may conflict not only with other values but with the agent's *interests*. This means there is still another sense in which suicide must be rational: it must be consistent with the suicidist's interests. If suicide is never in an agent's interests, suicide cannot be a rational act for the agent, even though it might be the most utile course of action from the perspective of others and at least consistent with her own values. The act might be rational as a sacrificial one, but that would not be suicide of the sort that concerns me.

With respect to the rationality of suicide, then, we have (1) a fundamental sense of rational that has to do with coherency, (2) a sense that has to do with utility, (3) a sense that has to do with discursive consistency, (4) a sense that has to do with judgmental and behavioral consistency, (5) a sense that has to do with consistency or compatibility with values, and (6) a sense that has to do with consistency or compatibility with interests. Minimally, we are concerned in the first case with whether it is intelligible to prefer and choose to die; whether, if one understands that death is personal annihilation, one can prefer and choose annihilation. In the second case we are asking whether suicide, as an act, is what most effectively achieves the agent's objectives. In the third case we are concerned with whether a potential suicidist deliberates in a proper and sound manner about taking her life. In the fourth case we are concerned with whether the judgment and decision to take her life would be invariably reached given the same values and circumstances. In the fifth case we are concerned with whether suicide, as an act, can be derived from, or is consistent with, whatever set of values an individual holds. And in the sixth case we are concerned with whether suicide can be one of the things an agent does to further her interests, or whether it always must be the greatest damage to those interests. And note that the sixth requirement, consistency with interests, may be at odds with the second, utility, since the agent's objectives may be counter to her interests. Suicide must be judged as something done against reason if its consequences are not really understood, if it is not the best course of action, if it is chosen by unsound means, if it is decided on in some idiosyncratic or perverse way, if it is at odds with what one prizes, or if it contravenes one's good. It should be added that "rational" also covers practical means-to-ends considerations, in the sense of whether the potential suicidist goes about killing herself in the most efficient and least painful way. However, I will not be concerned with this implemental sense.

All this talk of rationality makes a caveat necessary in anticipation of later discussion. I am not here endorsing some ahistorical notion of rationality. What follows turns on my being able to show preemptive suicide to be rational in the various senses just sketched. But to judge suicide rational in one or all of these senses is not necessarily to employ some ahistorical notion of rationality. It is, at least initially, simply to employ the reigning discursive standards which at present seem intuitive, such as internal consistency, truth of action-grounding beliefs, exclusion of seriously disruptive ambiguity, and entailment-compatibility among sets of propositions. These standards may be interpreted as ahistorical, or they may be interpreted as conventional or even as "conversational" in a Rortyan sense (Rorty, 1982), and arguments can be called for in support of each interpretation. For my purposes I can rely on received standards of coherency and rationality, however these may be thought to be grounded or even if the idea of their being grounded is rejected as wrong. At present we *do* make judgments about the rationality of suicide, even though they are generally negative judgments. I am trying to make out a case for judging preemptive suicide as rational by the same standards. This involves accepting and using present standards, and trying to show that they should be somewhat differently applied. It need not involve delving into the nature of those standards. As noted, I reject the relativistic extreme that would count suicide "rational" if merely consistent with the suicidist's values or perceived interests. But I also reject a doctrinaire "rationalist" or ahistorical position that would make the rationality or nonrationality of suicide an *a priori* matter determined by eternal canons. However, this is not the place to argue for or against either position. What I must do is make the best case I can for rational preemptive suicide. In this respect I am proceeding on a Davidsonian principle of generosity. Donald Davidson argues that for communication to be possible interlocutors must and do hold mostly true beliefs about their environment—and he does so without maintaining a traditional correspondence theory of truth, which would make the holding of true beliefs a simple matter of mirroring reality (Ramberg, 1989). I am assuming that in spite of lacking a universally accepted definition of rationality, we mostly agree on what is and is not rational—without rationality being an ahistorical reality we discern by necessity, nature, or luck. Our difficulties have less to do with what it is to be rational than with our willingness or unwillingness to count criteria for rationality satisfied in particular cases—particularly those which involve our values and interests.

A similar antiessentialist caveat is called for about agents' interests. Some interpret agents' interests objectively, drawing a hard distinction between interests and perceived interests; others reject the distinction and effectively make perceived interests exhaustive. I think a distinction can be made between what is in someone's interests and what that person believes is in her interests without introducing objective interests that carry metaphysical baggage like an inviolable human nature or essential good. My position is that if a potential suicidist and her peers judge suicide to be in her interests after cool, reflective consideration, including significantly successful efforts to gather and assess necessary data and enough time to ensure judgmental stability by avoidance of impulsive decisions, then that judgment would be sufficient. Some argue that it would still make sense to say that suicide is objectively not in the individual's interests, regardless of the judgment in question. I believe that the only way this claim can make sense is in the philosophically uninteresting case of something's not being known which, if known, would significantly affect deliberation. Since none of our interesting decisions can be made on the basis of certainty that all the facts are in, to require such certainty would be to preclude significant action. Interests are not purely conventional—and I will say in Chapters 4 and 5 how an interest in continued life is independent of convention or preference. But that does not mean that interests exist in a manner impervious to values and our best efforts at interpreting and assessing our situations. What brings up the idea of objective interests in the present context is the irrevocable nature of suicide, but to argue for objective interests is simply to beg the question against the rationality of suicide by taking the Cartesian position that regardless of how things look at any given time, suicide can never be judged in an agent's interests because always *possibly* not in her interests.

Something must now be said about the term "suicide" itself. Even though the term seems clear enough, addressing the question of whether we are capable of rationally choosing to die in less than extreme circumstances is made very difficult by entrenched attitudes that permeate the language we must use in our discussion. Without taking some care, what follows could suggest that I am only rationalizing something cowardly, selfish, and unnatural. "Suicide," like "murder," is a harsh term for the most final of acts: the taking of life. And, again like "murder," it bristles with moral opprobrium. In the case of murder, the moral censure is fully justified. But in the case of suicide, the matter is not so clear. The life taken is one's own, and there is at least an initial plausibility to the idea that one's own life is one's to take.

And it is problematic whether in committing suicide one does oneself harm in a straightforward enough way to merit present prohibitions. Killing, as opposed to murder, is deemed justified precisely when it is not murder, as when done in self-defense (there are also more questionable cases, such as legally sanctioned execution and acts of war). But generally our culture precludes that self-*killing* is ever anything but self-*murder*. This preclusion of suicidal justification is clearest when we consider the special cases wherein taking one's own life appears acceptable. Among these is that of a soldier choosing to die rather than reveal vital information to an enemy. But this sort of case is an exception to the wrongness of suicide mainly because it is normally not thought of as suicide at all. It is thought of as the *giving* of one's life when circumstances warrant such action. Were a soldier or spy to take a cyanide tablet or a bullet immediately on being captured, the action would almost certainly be thought suicidal and cowardly rather than heroic because of the assumption that the bullet or tablet was taken mainly to avoid the pain of torture or the ignominy of capture. Euthanatic suicide, because it involves the complicity of medical practitioners, is in a similar way usually not considered actually suicide. The stigma of suicide as a dishonorable act is avoided only in those cases where death is the sole alternative to an inexorable and insufferable alternative. But since human limitations prevent a situation's being known antecedently to be inexorable and insufferable, there is always room for doubt and acceptance of suicide is at best reluctant and tentative. As we shall see in Chapter 3, some go so far as to define suicide in a way that simply excludes cases where taking one's own life is deemed justifiable. At this point, then, one is tempted to introduce a neologism, or to make use of some current jargon or euphemism to discuss justifiable suicide. I think the temptations should be resisted. "Suicide" simply means "self-killing," and the term's connotations should not force one into artificiality. The only concession to make is to introduce qualifiers, as I have done in speaking of rational preemptive suicide, to denote the well-reasoned act of justifiably taking one's own life in less than extreme circumstances. It is also important to bear in mind that "suicide" means just that: *self-killing*. I am not concerned with death involving decisive and active participation by others.

With respect to the phrase "rational preemptive suicide," the bulk of what follows is, of course, an attempt to make out the senses of rational and preemptive, as well as to clarify the other senses mentioned. The key point is that "preemptive" as used here means that the sort of suicide which concerns me is not prompted by extreme circumstances such as terminal illness. As noted, I am not concerned with surcease suicide. The whole thrust of my project is to establish the rationality of ending one's own life well in advance of conditions which entail diminishment of self and loss of personal autonomy.

Final Preliminary Remarks

It may be necessary to mention that as ethical considerations are secondary to my project, legal considerations are tertiary and will receive little or no attention. Whatever the present legal situation, it must change if the general cultural view of suicide changes. Moreover, the main focus of legal considerations affecting the agent is necessarily on *attempted* suicide. With respect to the legal issue, what the potential suicidist must consider is whether her act will have disastrous legal consequences for her family or friends—for instance, prosecution for complicity or nonpayment of life insurance because of exceptional policy clauses. But I think these matters raise few interesting philosophical questions in the present context. Having said this about the legal aspect, I must also put aside a basically political matter to which the success or failure of my project is highly relevant. There would obviously be extremely important socio-economic benefits to a relatively large-scale practice of preemptive suicide in advanced age. Given the burden put on resources by a rapidly aging population, it is a hard but undeniable fact that *"suicide is cheap"* (Battin, 1987: 169; emphases in original). The cost of caring for and simply maintaining the lives of very elderly people is increasing alarmingly, and it will probably not be very long before there is some social pressure on the very elderly to follow practices we now associate with groups living under the most marginal conditions. An Inuit elder's wandering out on an ice floe, because she can no longer carry her weight in a community hard-pressed to survive, may come to be seen as socially responsible action

by our culture instead of as a barbaric practice. I realize that
my project will be attractive to pragmatic governments and
other tough-minded policy groups. However, my interest in
the beneficial socio-economic consequences of suicide is limited
to how they may figure in an individual's suicidal deliberation.
My concern is with individual decision, not with public policy.
Preemptive suicide in advanced age must be shown to be a
rational option before we can consider whether public policies
should support and promote it. But it is not my intention to
dismiss ethical, religious, legal, or economic considerations. The
point is that this study is concerned with the most fundamental
question about suicide: whether it is rational to take one's life.
If suicide is always against one's values, and/or is always the
worst harm one can do oneself, then self-inflicted death is never
rationally justified, regardless of misconceived ethical, religious,
legal, or social endorsement or its attractiveness to policy-makers.
In any case, questions about the rationality of suicide are complex
enough, and can best be dealt with if I "bracket" issues which,
if addressed, would render my project practically impossible. I
shall argue that suicide is sometimes in one's interests, in being
the prevention of anticipated (worse) harm, and hence that it is
coherent to prefer to die at an advanced age. If that basic point
can be established, then the ethical, social, legal, economic, and
religious questions can be taken in their turn.

In closing this chapter, I must warn the reader that the
difficulty and elusiveness of many of the points I need to
make will require some repetition—as is already evident. But it
is not simple repetition. What is required is that numerous points
be made in slightly different ways and from slightly different
perspectives. The question of suicide is not only complex, it is
emotionally loaded, and one cost of clarity in what follows is
repetition. I turn now to how advanced age introduces reasons
for contemplating suicide, reasons analogous to those introduced
by terminal illness. It is necessary to say in detail what prompts
consideration of rational preemptive suicide—especially since it
is central to my claims that consideration of suicide need not
be prompted only by hopelessly desperate circumstances. In the
next chapter I shall consider how one may come to realize that
"the time for Yes has passed."

2

THE EPISTEMOLOGICAL CRISIS OF AGING

Some become too old even for their truths.

Nietzsche, *Zarathustra*

The common view is that any philosophical issues aging raises concern only the social implications of growing old and are essentially ethical. Acknowledged issues usually include access to medical resources by the aged, criterial and policy questions regarding familial and public obligations for care and support, and questions about the extent of diagnostic candor owed those whose lives are ending. These are largely problems raised *by* the aged for the younger. Nonetheless, it is true that the philosophical issues generated are mostly subsumable under the broad banner of ethics. Where the focus is on the aging individual's own problems and adjustments, the issues are more practical and have to do with helping the elderly cope with age-related difficulties—for instance, by provision of educational programs, various assistance schemes, and transportation. This latter sort of issue is rightly thought to be rarely of philosophical interest. But contrary to the common view, aging itself raises epistemological questions for the aging individual. In particular, it raises questions about possible growing unreliability of reasoning and about more certain decreases in interpretive adaptiveness—decreases which occur in spite of the novelty and diversity of experience we accumulate in growing older (Prado, 1983, 1986). These epistemological questions are extremely important to what I can best describe as the preservation of the individual's intellectuality in advanced age. The questions are less about delineable afflictions than they are about holistic changes for the worse. And for some, these changes pose a much more ominous and exigent threat than do the more familiar maladies which characterize old age. These maladies may cause their bearer great discomfort or even chronic pain, but the intellectual changes in question are changes to the individual's most essential aspects: they are changes in the very thought processes that make an individual the person she is. And perhaps even more importantly, they are changes in the attitudes and sensibilities that define her as a subject of experience. These negative changes also affect the individual's reflective understanding of her own attitudes and sensibilities, and so hamper or vitiate efforts at adjustment. In what follows I will speak of the "reflective aging individual," and mean a person at least older than sixty-five who is perspicaciously self-aware, whose intellectual self-awareness shapes and defines her existence as a person and a social entity, and who values her intellectual capacities enough to be seriously concerned that age may erode them in various ways—especially in ways not evident to her. (In referring to an aging individual whose reflectiveness and perspicacity are moot or not immediately relevant, I shall use a more common phrase such as "elderly person.") The reflective aging individual is one who equates serious erosion of her reasoning, her interpretive flexibility, and her perspicacious self-awareness, with distortion or loss of personal identity, and so with a kind of death.

The essence of the epistemological issues raised by aging for the reflective individual is that the very nature of the erosion of intellectual proficiency is self-masking. Erosion of reasoning and interpretive adaptiveness naturally includes disruption of reliable assessment of conclusions reached and construals imposed on events. Serious deterioration of reasoning and interpretive capacity is at best sporadically evident to the afflicted individual. Moreover, decline of effective self-awareness disrupts effective monitoring of one's own reasoning and formation of construals of situations. If deterioration of this sort is even suspected to be inherent to advanced age, then the reflective aging individual faces the inescapable epistemological difficulty of having to doubt her abilities to reason and interpret productively and to assess her own reasoning, attitudes, and priorities. Our apparently limitless capacity for rationalization and self-deception worsens her difficulty because these not only slow recognition of deterioration, they insure that even when she realizes something is amiss the reflective aging individual will tend to respond ineffectually, postponing hard decisions until it is too late to make them. And they raise the specter of wholly unrecognized decline. In terms of bare survival, rationalization and self-deception are all very well, for a reduced individual is able to continue living without suffering the crippling despondency which would be caused by full realization of intellectual diminishment. But for anyone to whom bare survival is insufficient, the possibility of masked diminishment is an extremely frightening one. It raises pressing questions about how we might continue to reliably assess our level of intellectual competence, and about what we can and might do if we believe that competence to be threatened or declining. And in this way the possibility of diminishment, whether evident or masked, prompts the bleakest realization, namely, that it may be preferable to end a life that can continue only in a sadly and unacceptably reduced way.

Changes

Even the healthiest and most favored among us are neither as quick or strong nor as resilient or adaptive at seventy years of age as at twenty. Physical deterioration is obvious and, though now more controlled by better nutrition and improved medical treatment, has yet to be reversed. Less obvious but just as real are mental changes for the worse. While aging is not simply a matter of wholesale and persistent deterioration, we must recognize that as complex organisms we do degenerate in various ways and at varying rates. While vocabulary, articulateness, and comprehension are only slightly diminished by age seventy-five, cognitive efficiency may be down by forty per-cent due to slowness of uptake and response. One in ten of those sixty-five and over shows organic brain disorder. So-called "normal" age-related neural deterioration begins in the frontal lobes, which means that even where there is no clinical condition, and even where there is no appreciable decline in purely cognitive capacity, there will almost certainly be personality or psychological changes such as heightened emotionality and self-centeredness. Often psychological changes are ignorantly conflated with impairment of reasoning, which is quite different and usually pathological when evident. Someone whose moods and attitudes have changed markedly for the worse may still be able to reason as well as ever. But psychological changes, in affecting moods and attitudes, affect the motives, priorities, values, and goals that reasoning serves. So the difference between deteriorative changes in reasoning and psychological changes is less important than it might seem, because psychological changes indirectly cripple even undiminished reasoning ability by insuring it is always badly used. In addition to fairly readily described psychological changes, there are no doubt ultimately neurophysiological but less easily categorized changes: concentration is impeded, attention spans are shortened, and memory notoriously grows less reliable. The efficiency of thought declines due to a general slowing of the process. Some of these negative changes may be due merely to lack of challenge and practice, or to the distraction of chronic ailments, but their reality is undeniable. And this is to say nothing of the onset of major afflictions such as acute confusion, the early stages of Alzheimer's, arteriosclerotic dementia, and depressive illness—all of which affect reasoning and emotions long before they become serious enough to be diagnosable. So while there is no strong evidence that sheer reasoning ability deteriorates prior to the onset of significant senility, there are factors that muddle the thinking process long before that stage is reached. For complex reasons, then, advanced age itself constitutes grounds to question abilities which previously were questioned only in case of odd and inexplicable behavior. Even if an aging individual's reasoning remains unimpaired, and her interpretive adaptiveness—her flexibility in construing what is going on—is undiminished, her very age must occasion doubts or at least unease about those abilities (Tierney, 1982; Henig, 1981; Denny, 1979; Hoffmeister, 1979; Jarvik, 1979; Birren and Schaie, 1977; Birren, 1968a, 1968b; Siegler, 1976; Baltes and Schaie, 1974; Bromley, 1974; Botwinick, 1967).

For my present purposes, changes in reasoning ability are actually of secondary importance. This is because my interest is in a stage of advanced age at which an individual must be still capable of deciding whether or not she should go on living, and so still be capable of effective reasoning. Once loss of reasoning has occurred, the aging individual is past the stage at which suicide could be preemptive and rational. Even if there is intermittent unimpaired reasoning and realization of the partial loss of that ability, decisions taken in those moments of clarity simply would not be reliable enough for suicidal deliberation and action. Like terminal illness, reasoning is something about which we can be concerned productively only in an anticipatory way (this cruel fact is what supports the popular but quite mistaken idea that so long as sanity is questioned it can be assumed intact). Contrary to the all-or-nothing requirement for unimpaired reasoning, even fairly serious loss of interpretive adaptiveness does not necessarily preclude responsible suicidal deliberation, decision, and action. Others cannot help us reason. They may help us reason more effectively, so long as we retain our ability to reason. But they cannot help us once that ability has deteriorated, not in a way that would make steps followed and conclusions reached *our* steps and conclusions. However, others *can* help us reconstrue and better understand situations, reorder priorities, and reconsider our attitudes, aims, and objectives. As noted in the preceding chapter, reliance on consultation is crucial for the aging potential suicidist, and she may still profit from it even after significant loss of interpretive adaptiveness. The crucial consideration is that the loss of interpretive adaptiveness not be extreme or pathological and irreversible. However, this hopeful note requires elaborate qualification. Even though not accompanied by loss of reasoning, loss of interpretive adaptiveness means that the aging individual is hampered in recognizing changes in herself and others and in usefully structuring and understanding novel situations. She is less able to cope with those changes and situations. For example, she may grow increasingly unable to appreciate how difficulties with others are due to entrenched or obsessive attitudes or behavior on her part. This is bad enough when loss of interpretive adaptiveness is real. But awareness of the *possibility* of masked or unrecognized loss of interpretive adaptiveness—or of reasoning, for that matter—will have similar deleterious effects by undermining the aging individual's every assessment and conclusion. And this is especially true of her self-assessments. So even if interpretive adaptiveness has not declined, it may be systematically undercut and frustrated by pernicious doubt. Therefore, whether or not there has been decline of interpretive adaptiveness, or at least some actual decline is still reversible, the willing help and reassurance of others may prove insufficient for the aging individual to cope effectively or to trust her construals and conclusions. The point here goes beyond the question of interpretive adaptiveness. The reflective aging individual understands that even if her reasoning and interpretive adaptiveness are drastically impaired, it may appear to her that nothing has changed. There is nothing she can do; she must bear the hollow knowledge that she will not know her own unreason. But the truly shattering realization is that she will not be able to tell *when* unreason begins. So there will be a time when fear and suspicion of decline will jeopardize all serious thought. This is why the reflective aging individual's difficulties are not simply psychological or clinical. They are epistemological in kind because they are doubts about her reason and interpretive adaptiveness that may be entertained while these capacities are still unimpaired. The deteriorative changes age brings pose epistemological questions because by being real, seriously deteriorative, and unrealized in some cases, they are possibly so in any given case.

Nor are the epistemological questions only abstract ones which can more often than not be set aside while life mainly goes on as before. To the extent that negative changes in reasoning and interpretive adaptiveness are suspected or evident to the individual in whom they occur, and to the extent that they are reflected or assumed in how others treat her, those changes or their perception have a cumulative effect that does more than pose philosophical questions. At many points in our lives our conception of who and what we are, our self–image, is shaped and reshaped by adjustments we make to specific successes and failures. But in advanced age that image is reshaped by a global—though usually gradual—reassessment of our capacities.

And the crucial point about this reassessment is that it cannot be preliminary to efforts at long-term improvement. The whole point is that the reassessment has to do with understanding what we are *becoming*, not with responding to something that has gone wrong and can be set right. The reassessment faced in advanced age does not call for even massive adjustment to limitations, as might earlier recognition that we are not as strong as we might like or as bright as we hoped. It requires not so much adjustment, for that suggests possible correction, as a kind of basic realignment of who and what we are. What is needed is less an acclimation of more or less specific expectations to fairly delineated limitations, than a reorientation of the individual's very self. The required reorientation can be effectively characterized by considering one of its central components: recognition of loss of facility for a certain *level* of thought. Like a concert violinist who, though she continues to play, ceases to be a professional violinist when afflicted with arthritis, an aging individual of course continues to think, but may cease to be a thinker of a certain order because of age-related changes—changes which need not be due to a pathological condition as in the violinist's case. The aging individual then has to accommodate herself to the realization that certain levels of thought have not only become unattainable, they may become unrecognizable to her for reasons that still fall short of the sorts of conditions we would characterize as clinical. Unlike the arthritic violinist, the person whose anatomical flexibility is quite markedly reduced at seventy-five from what it was at twenty-five is not pathologically afflicted: she is simply an aged organism. But her flexibility is nonetheless reduced. In the same way, a person may be a long way from being senile and still have lost her aptitude for even moderately abstract thought or, more importantly, a certain order of rigorous and penetrating self–reflection. But her *experienced* loss is not softened by its benign nature, nor is the difficulty she has in accepting what she cannot deny. Bertrand Russell somewhere said that he had never thought as abstractly as when he was collaborating with Alfred North Whitehead in writing *Principia Mathematica* (Russell and Whitehead, 1910–13), and his admission was sad because of the implication that he never would again. And it is not difficult to imagine Russell, toward the end of his very long life and when immersed in the antinuclear movement, reflecting that what he and Whitehead valued so highly so many years before was really of little import. Russell probably anticipated that development, recognizing that the level of abstract thought he had once attained might not only be lost to him as an exercisable capacity, but also as an object of recognition and appreciation. The more Russell valued abstract thought, the harder it would be for him to acknowledge that double loss, and the harder it would be for him to be sanguine about his future as an intellectual entity. A reflective person who is aware of the unfortunate nature of changes beginning in later life may envisage a time when she will no longer value not only the intellectuality she prizes, but the level of self-awareness and self-understanding she has achieved, and the openness of mind which goes with that achievement. Reorientation of self in old age, then, goes well beyond abstract epistemological questions to reflection on how age changes us for the worse at the deepest levels of our being, and so prompts the soberest thoughts about the value of continued existence.

Nonetheless, many will reject out of hand the idea that the considerations outlined above properly occasion serious thought of suicide. It will be argued that the intellectual aspect of our nature is being given exaggerated importance. And it will be denied that there are adequate grounds to anticipate the sort of deterioration described. It is fashionable now to reject as misconceived the view that age inevitably brings serious holistic deterioration. The belief that it does is blamed on cultural factors, and old age—at least as now conceived—is itself described as a cultural creation. Much of what I have said will be suspect and even offensive to many who will see it as founded on baseless fear and obsessively focused on a disproportionate evaluation of a single dimension of human life. To those who think in this way, there simply are no epistemological problems peculiar to aging, though there certainly are numerous characteristic difficulties. I think I understand the point of view in question, because I held it for some time. Most of my earlier work on aging was directed toward breaking down stereotypic thinking about advanced age and the aged. In *Rethinking How We Age* (Prado, 1986) and elsewhere I used the idea that some age-related decline in interpretive adaptiveness is due to learned, practical factors, arguing against stereotypic views of aging as inherently deteriorative. I even sketched a form of therapy for the reversal of adaptive or interpretive decline (Prado, 1986: 132–37). I still think some interpretive difficulties that attend old age are practical, but I no longer believe that is enough to render aging any the less destructive. One of the most difficult things to do, at any age, is to rigorously examine our construals of whatever we encounter, from situations involving others to our own most private experiences. So any decrease of interpretive adaptiveness must be one of the most worrying things to encounter or suspect in oneself. The reflective aging individual may well see recognition or even significant suspicion of decreasing interpretive adaptiveness as the beginning of the end of her existence as a competent intellectual entity. And failure to see that as a reason to consider preemptive suicide is something I can only attribute to either ideological commitments or a kind of aspect-blindness. I will return below to the matter of appreciating the propriety of suicidal consideration, but at this juncture I must pursue the loss of interpretive adaptiveness. And to better understand the loss in question, we have to get clearer on the nature of interpretive adaptiveness. This can best be done by considering the sort *not* due to psychological or neurological deterioration. Practical decline of interpretive adaptiveness does not require complex technical exposition for basic understanding precisely because it is something we all do as part of ordering experience.

Interpretive Parsimony

In "Ageing and Narrative" (Prado, 1983) I introduced the notion of "interpretive parsimony" to explain how some age-related interpretive difficulties are the consequences of *learned* interpretive practices, and not the effects of neurophysiological deterioration on our adaptive capacities. Even though practical in nature, interpretive parsimony may be as obstructive as a pathological condition. And it may be even more odious to the aging individual who recognizes it as unavoidable even though not pathological. Basically, interpretive parsimony is extension to a counterproductive degree of the necessary activity of organizing experience, and it may affect and condition everything from elemental conceptualization of objects in one's environment, through understanding of what another person is doing, to the most complex interpretive activity—as in the case of a theoretical scientist gerrymandering anomalous experimental results to fit theoretical expectations. At whatever level of application, interpretive parsimony is the employment of, and reliance on, too few, too rigid, and excessively anticipatory construals of events and people and their actions—including oneself and one's own actions. It is not my intent to rehearse what I have said elsewhere, but there are three basic points that need to be made about interpretive parsimony: First, even though interpretive economy is familiar to us as stereotypic thinking and the dominance of habitual expectations and responses, my term designates a more unified pattern than do terms designating more familiar but diversely identified behavioral patterns. When we consider restricted and restrictive ways of thinking and acting, we tend to do so in terms of specific practices. For instance, we tend to consider stereotypic thinking primarily in connection with racial prejudice, and the dominance of attitudinal habit is usually thought of in connection with adaptive difficulties of a narrow sort, such as learning new job procedures. We rarely think and speak of such practices as elements of extensive, integrated, and complex behavior patterns. When we do so, it is invariably in connection with people who manifest *extraordinary* inflexibility of mind. What we fail to see is that such cases are only notable extremes of interpretive parsimony, not different and limited phenomena. Second, while interpretive parsimony is a most useful notion in enabling us to understand some attitudinal and behavioral changes in the elderly as the cumulative effect of economy of construal, it also forces us to realize that we unknowingly collaborate with psychological and neurophysiological deterioration in the undermining of our adaptive capacities. That is, we add learned restrictions to those imposed on us by deterioration. This means that while our most recently identified prejudice, namely, agism (Levin and Levin, 1980), has no *adequate* basis in fact, chronological age nonetheless may be a better ground for negative attitudes toward the elderly than we would like (McKee, 1988: 133). Third, and most importantly, interpretive parsimony increases because of *success*. That is, given our fairly stable environment, we manage surprisingly well with narrower and fewer interpretive practices than we might ideally employ. Parsimonious construals of people and their actions often are adequate for our purposes, even though not generous enough for truly productive understanding of others and rewarding interaction with them. Rather than experience forcing us to broaden our interpretive practices as we age, we seem to force experience to fit our practices. This is the essence of interpretive parsimony, and because of relative success, this interpretive economy increases to a point where we no longer deal effectively with the people we encounter. We address and hear characters largely of our own making, and mainly live through events we shape to fit our expectations. As Patrick McKee points out in commenting on interpretive parsimony, we seem to be "left in old age with a pronounced tendency . . . to see the world in narrower terms" (McKee, 1988: 133).

The worrying point about practical interpretive or adaptive decline is that it is as generally certain as physical decline in spite of not being a consequence of the latter. Recognition of growing interpretive parsimony, then, will not be reassuring recognition of a practical problem to be set right by changes in one's habits. Instead, the recognition of interpretive parsimony is one of the chief elements of the crisis the reflective person faces in advanced age. Whatever reassurance there may be in the fact that interpretive loss is not always pathological will be compensated for by realization that, whatever its causes, it cannot be everywhere identified and reversed. However, recognition of interpretive parsimony is in no way as certain as recognition of physical decline.

The parsimonious restriction of what we make of people and events around us, as well as of our relations to those people and our place in those events, inevitably gives rise to occasions in which interaction with others proves frustrating or unproductive. But these situations will be dismissed by most people with *more* stereotypic thinking of precisely the sort that led to the situations in the first place. If interaction with someone goes wrong, the fault will be attributed to just the parsimonious stereotypic characteristics which—operant in one person and recognized by the other—produced the specific communicative discordance in the first place. For example, if an older individual treats a younger one in a manner indicating to the younger that she is being assumed ignorant, the younger person may behave curtly or impatiently. Then the older person, rather than consider whether her own behavior prompted the rudeness or impatience, will be confirmed in her belief that all young people are ignorant—and disrespectful to boot. The result is that an occasion for recognition of interpretive parsimony is lost.

Benign memory loss is for the most part the only negative mental change commonly and readily recognized as a function of age and accepted by both those afflicted and others with a fair measure of equanimity. Our culture actually promotes tolerant recognition and acknowledgement of benign memory loss—largely through humor (Palmore, 1971). It does so for pragmatic reasons. For one thing, people whose memories are less than reliable must be alerted against trusting their memories in order that they not disrupt the smooth flow of social interaction. And they must be prepared to be dealt with in special ways. It is notable how our culture permits a measure of repetition and insistence regarding the arrangement of meeting-times and places with elderly people that would be considered rude if used with younger people (notice the tone a doctor's receptionist uses when making appointments for elderly patients). Most aging individuals readily admit to benign memory loss and do not see it as demeaning or debilitating in itself, though they may see it as a harbinger of more personally diminishing changes to come. But in spite of the readiness of the young to question the old's construals of events and situations, most older people seem to actually consider their interpretive adaptiveness to be *improved* by age and "experience." They are seldom prepared to seriously question its reliability, even while admitting they are becoming "set in their ways." The apparent inconsistency evaporates when we understand that the imagined improvement is thought to occur in specific areas of special importance—areas usually having to do with human behavior and motivation.

In the case of the reflective aging individual, recognition of interpretive parsimony is considerably likelier than in the case of individuals not given to introspection. Interpretive parsimony may be recognized by a reflective individual in such cases as the foregoing example, when the behavior of those with whom she interacts begins to fall systematically short of her expectations or is otherwise seriously puzzling, raising questions about why those others should respond as they do. Interpretive parsimony may also be recognized by a reflective individual on occasions when her *own* behavior fails to meet her expectations or is otherwise seriously puzzling, raising questions about what hidden motives may be operant. In the first sort of case, because the person in question is reflective, she will not be satisfied to dismiss how she is treated by others as due entirely to their own perceptions and biases. She will consider that she may be somehow eliciting perplexing responses. If she is treated condescendingly, she will ponder whether she has acted in some way that invites condescension. In the second sort of case, the reflective person will look more closely at her own motives and intentions when she surprises herself with an overly hasty judgment about someone or some situation. Precisely because interpretive parsimony is learned, and practical, it is accessible to reflection in a way that decreased interpretive adaptiveness due to neurophysiological deterioration is not—though the latter may be intermittently recognized. If a reflective person realizes she has grown interpretively parsimonious, and she understands the learned and practical nature of interpretive parsimony, she may initially feel confidence in her ability to assess her parsimony with a view to reversing it. Against this, if a reflective person realizes she has suffered neurophysiological deterioration, and understands the nature of that deterioration, she will have no illusions about her ability to reverse that deterioration. However, there is actually little reason to think that interpretive parsimony is finally any more manageable than neurological deterioration (McKee, 1988). For one thing, assessment and efforts to reverse interpretive parsimony turn on interaction with others providing the impetus and material for reflection on what underlies both our behavior toward them and their consequent behavior toward us. And productive interaction of the required sort tends to decrease in frequency and depth as those with whom the elderly interact grow more distant because of their own interpretive parsimony. But the central problem, as indicated earlier, is that there is an extremely difficult criterial question generated by self-assessment of adaptive capacities. Regardless of the greater likelihood that a reflective person may *recognize* interpretive parsimony in herself, it is by no means as likely that she will be able to deal effectively with it. In fact, recognition will more likely lead to greater self-doubt and frustration—and in that way further impede her interaction with others. If there is recognition and acknowledgement of interpretive parsimony, the reflective aging individual will find herself in a profound quandary as to what she can do about it; a quandary made more difficult still by the growing interpretive rigidity which occasioned it. As said above, the changes age brings pose epistemological questions and affect the aging individual's self-image in pressing ways. Far from being merely abstract considerations, they in effect constitute a crisis of confidence and, eventually, a crisis of identity.

Epistemological Crises

Alisdair MacIntyre introduced the notion of an epistemological crisis in considering how someone may fail to understand what is taking place around her, and do so in a serious and paralyzing way. MacIntyre contends that an individual may be at a complete loss as to what to do because she realizes there are systematically different and mutually exclusive interpretations of an important situation she faces. She may become aware "of the existence of alternative and rival schemata, which yield mutually incompatible accounts of what is going on . . . " (MacIntyre, 1977: 454). Using Hamlet's predicament on his return to Elsinore as an apt fictive example, MacIntyre remarks that what Hamlet finds on his return from Wittenberg poses a crisis because there are "too many schemata available for interpreting the events at Elsinore . . . There is the revenge schema of the Norse sagas; there is the renaissance courtier's schema; there is a Machiavellian schema about competition for power" (MacIntyre, 1977: 454). Hamlet does not know whether to believe his mother, Rosencrantz and Guildenstern, or his father's ghost about what has occurred. He looks for corroborative evidence for one or another interpretation, but until Hamlet "has adopted some schema he does not know what to treat as evidence." And equally, "until he knows what to treat as evidence he cannot tell what schema to adopt" (MacIntyre, 1977: 454). The resolution of the epistemological crisis cannot be a matter of choosing among competing schemata by having recourse to "the facts," because what *count* as facts are a function of whatever interpretive schema is operant. The epistemological crisis is not a matter of not knowing enough; it is a matter of not knowing what to make of what is available.

The epistemological crisis may go deeper than the need to make sense of particular events. The crisis can also be a crisis of self-identity. Interpretive schemata are not employed by autonomous Cartesian egos. The interpretive schemata we use not only shape and define who others are and what they are up to, they shape and define who *we* are and what *we* are up to. MacIntyre sees in Shakespeare's account of Hamlet's epistemological crisis what Descartes' account of his own crisis "altogether misses, for Shakespeare invites us to reflect on the crisis of the self as a crisis in the tradition which has formed the self." Hamlet's crisis occurs in the context of his history. Against this, Descartes "invented an unhistorical . . . self-consciousness and trie[d] to describe his [own] epistemological crisis in terms of it" (MacIntyre, 1977: 459). The Cartesian crisis is a matter of a self being momentarily problematic with respect to its existence, but its occasion is crucially artificial. The crisis is prompted by philosophical speculation, not by real doubt. The "crisis" is an intellectual ploy to introduce a metaphysical entity: a substantive self which, once "proven" to exist, is established as essentially unchanging and self-contained. It is the Cartesian ego's self-containment that enabled Descartes' malevolent demon to be defeated, because that demon challenged detachable beliefs held by an enduring entity. In this way the Cartesian ego was never really jeopardized; what were jeopardized were its beliefs conceived of as so many extraneous items. MacIntyre's epistemological crisis is posed by a very different demon, one we might call the "malevolent hermeneut." The malevolent hermeneut challenges not particular beliefs, but the interpretive schema within which something *is* a belief and, more importantly, within which *someone is a subject*. In challenging that schema, the malevolent hermeneut challenges the functional identity of the interpreting self. And since it is realization that there are competing construals of a given situation that precipitates the epistemological crisis, the malevolent hermeneut need only force us to acknowledge the possibility of significant interpretive alternatives to paralyze us with indecision. The subject of the epistemological crisis is unable to act until she can act on the basis of one or another interpretation. And because we are not Cartesian egos capable of existing in some pure sense, when she is unable to act she begins to lose her identity. She cannot even continue as a passive subject, because to be a subject is to interpret what happens to her in some particular way. As MacIntyre goes on to say in considering Hamlet's epistemological crisis, a subject's identity is determined by the complex narrative which organizes her life. If that narrative is sufficiently disrupted in the epistemological crisis, the subject's identity is rendered as uncertain as her understanding of the problematic events which initiated her doubts. Because she is unable to adopt an explanatory schema to construe the events in question in one or another way, the subject of the epistemological crisis finds her interpretive practices themselves suddenly problematic, and that in turn jeopardizes the *persona* those practices define.

The epistemological crisis, then, is an interpretive failure and consequent paralysis resulting from the unresolved need to choose among alternative situation-construals, each of which is pressing in its own way. And if the crisis is serious enough, the subject's inability to deal with the events that prompt the crisis renders problematic the very mechanisms she uses to interpret events. If that happens, the interpreting subject cannot function, cannot *be* a subject, and the interpretive crisis becomes a crisis of identity. These extreme cases perhaps go beyond what MacIntyre envisaged, but they are precisely the cases that concern us. Like MacIntyre, Robert Kastenbaum has described an interpretive crisis which he calls the "crisis of explanation" in old age. Kastenbaum builds on empirical data, which show that elderly people usually do not know how to deal with old age, to argue that the self-identity of the elderly is threatened by interpretive difficulties. He tells us that many elderly persons *"literally do not know what has happened to them, cannot explain to themselves . . . who they are, and cannot determine in which direction to move and for what purpose"* (Kastenbaum, 1964: 321, emphases in original). The aging individual's crisis is considerably worse than Hamlet's. It is not prompted by an interpretive quandary raised by a set of events which, while capable of prompting the epistemological crisis, are fairly circumscribed and usually external to the individual. The aging individual's entire life-organizing schema fails because of changes in herself and how she comes to be treated by others in every aspect of life. The crisis of explanation can be understood as having several stages, though they are not necessarily temporally sequential. First, the aging individual realizes that she "can't go on" (Blythe, 1979: 5), that she can no longer live her life with a horizonless future. Second, she begins to find her own attitudes and behavior as unreliable as she is beginning to find her memory. For instance, she may be surprised at her new sentimentality or obsessive concern with her health. Third, she is dealt with differently by others—as less responsible and with vaguely problematic thought and action. Then, as in the case of a scientist who at some point can no longer accommodate the experimental anomalies of an unviable theory, the aging individual no longer can accommodate anomalies in both her own attitudes and behavior and how she is treated. At that point her interpretive schema fails, and she cannot sustain the identity that schema defines. The very identity her interpretive practices presuppose and delineate is what becomes most precarious when those practices become suspect and especially when that identity ceases to be accepted by others. Recognition that one is growing old is certainly prompted by changes in oneself, but those changes need not, of themselves, prompt a crisis of explanation. For one thing, that recognition is piecemeal and gradual. The crisis is more likely and more compellingly prompted by changes in how one is treated. Malcolm Cowley says that "We start by growing old in other people's eyes, then slowly we come to share their judgment" (Cowley, 1982: 5). The aging person finds herself treated by others in a manner too much at odds with her expectations for her to in turn deal with those others as she takes them to be—and to do so as the person she takes *herself* to be. For a time her interpretive schema can be adjusted, but as in the case of a theory burdened with too many qualifications, it soon becomes unworkable. As Kastenbaum puts it, the aging individual comes not to know who she is, because the person she has taken herself to be is not only undermined by her own occasionally puzzling behavior, it is no longer acknowledged by most of those with whom she deals.

The connection between the epistemological crisis and the crisis of explanation is mainly a matter of degree and the measure of reflective awareness. The crisis of explanation escalates into an epistemological crisis when experienced by a reflective person who understands that the crisis of explanation is posed by interpretive failure, is generated by interpretive conflicts, and calls for adoption of a new identity-defining and life-organizing schema. Whereas an unreflective person may accept her puzzlement and frustration as part of whatever is happening to her, and adapt to her circumstances in a way I discuss in the next section, the reflective person will appreciate that she is being treated according to one or another of her culture's stereotypes of the aged, and that she must rethink her situation. She must assess to what extent the stereotypes apply, and how she may best acknowledge irremediable changes and improve the still-manageable aspects of her situation. But rather than reduce her difficulties, her understanding may only make matters worse. Recognition of stereotypic thinking applied to herself invites parsimonious interpretation of disruptive incidents as due to stereotypic thinking on the part of others. Because it is threateningly diminishing of self, the possibility that the stereotyping has some real basis may be shunned. This tends to isolate the aging individual, to entrench unproductive views and attitudes, and to superficially and temporarily ease her crisis with facile defiance. The result can be an escalation of her crisis into an even more crippling one. The very reflectiveness that insures recognition of stereotypic thinking affords an almost irresistible opportunity for self-deception. In trying to deal with what she will see as unfair stereotyping of herself by others, the reflective aging individual may enter a sort of self-bargaining stage. She may concede a certain amount of reason for worry, but insist on construing most of the changes which elicit the unwelcome behavior on the part of others as positive rather than deteriorative. She may see those changes as products of growth and new wisdom rather than decline. For example, she may see an increase in self-centeredness not as a product of negative attitudinal and emotive changes, but as finally giving herself her due; she may accept a narrowing of interests and perspectives as a new focusing on what is truly important. She will in effect try to construct a new narrative in which she is "not getting older, just getting better," as Madison Avenue would have it. (See Williams, 1986a, 1986b, 1984, for parallels in chronic illness.) These partial concessions and reconstruals are misguided efforts to work out a new interpretive schema, and though misguided, may be successful for a time. However, they are extremely dangerous maneuvers. First, they introduce greater cognitive dissonance. Second, they virtually insure that the reflective aging individual will either become more confirmed in her misconstruals, and so more isolated, or finally face a more devastating crisis. Third, because they are essentially no more than postponements of the inevitable, the time they buy could well leave the individual with no scope for the hard decisions she should eventually make.

Settling for Senility

A person facing Kastenbaum's crisis of explanation in old age, whether or not she is a reflective individual, is under tremendous psychological pressure to "explain" her situation, to adopt an interpretive schema that resolves her crisis. But she will be loathe to confront the fact that it is *she* who is changing. And because few are equal to the task of understanding, let alone dealing with, large-scale failure and revision of an interpretive schema, the aging individual will strongly tend to look for something external to herself to explain what has happened—as she would look for the causes of an affliction. Kastenbaum remarks that many elderly people see old age as a misfortune, almost as if with luck it might have been avoided (Kastenbaum, 1964: 321). The aging individual sees herself as someone whom something has *befallen*, rather than as someone in the process of natural transformation. And this means that the crisis of explanation is prone to be half-resolved by adoption of one or another of our culture's stereotypic schemata. The dominant schema, which we can dub the "senility script," supports the view of advanced age as affliction. And it is the schema most likely to be adopted by the perplexed aging individual in lieu of more productive—but much harder—resolution of her crisis of explanation by acceptance that she has aged to a point calling for radical reappraisal of who and what she is. In other words, the aging individual is most likely to accept her culture's dominant stereotype and unknowingly adopt as her self-defining narrative precisely the senility script imposed on her by others. People do not usually think of their thought and action as functions of the employment of interpretive schemata. When the aging individual realizes that something has gone seriously wrong, when anomalies begin to pile up, she will not be prepared to recognize that her interpretive schema has failed because it served and defined a different—a younger—person. Instead the aging individual will be inclined to accept redefinition by her youth-oriented culture. The basis for this acquiescence was established in her own youth, when she internalized the same monolithic stereotype of old age which is now applied to her. That stereotype casts old age as a time of inevitable and holistic decline, as necessarily a time of decreasing autonomy and responsibility. The stereotype precludes the possibility of the aging individual making significant decisions about herself and her prospects and condemns her to dependency and sufferance. As Phillida Salmon tells us: "the official psychology . . . portrays the old in terms of deficiency and personal deterioration, . . . elderly people are not given a voice in defining their condition" (Salmon, 1985: 41). And the ready-made schema diminishes the aging individual in her own eyes as it diminishes her in the eyes of others. Nonetheless, abhorrent though it may be, the senility script our culture offers at least furnishes the aged person with the interpretive schema she so desperately needs, so it is unthinkingly adopted and used to self-define herself into a sad and powerless old age. The damage done is just what Salmon notes: the old are deprived of a voice in saying who they are and what their lives might be like. And what is most significant in the present context is that adoption of the senility script robs the old of the chance of forgoing the worst parts of those lives by committing preemptive suicide. The elderly person is denied the opportunity to assess her situation and prospects by being made to take herself as a victim of affliction, rather than as a person changing in ways which she cannot prevent but has the ability to avoid.

At present our culture's contribution to an elderly person's epistemological and psychological struggles with old age is pressure to accept one of two standing interpretive schemata. The first of these is the dominant schema just described, whose intellectual parent is Aristotle, and which has an aging person deteriorating—equally and inexorably—in every aspect of her being. The alternative schema, whose intellectual parent is Cicero and which is gaining favor, is greatly more optimistic. In its contemporary "constructionist" incarnation it conceives of old age as a cultural product and—barring diagnosable clinical conditions—denies that advanced age brings systematic deteriorative mental changes. But in spite of the attractiveness of this second schema, both schemata are unacceptable because of their simplistic nature. The first facilely generalizes about an extremely complex process and glosses very real differences among individuals. Worst of all, it yokes autonomy and respon- sibleness to chronological age so that the soundness of an elderly person's assessments and decisions is rendered problematic *prior* to any symptoms of senescence (Prado, 1986; Levin and Levin, 1980; Palmore, 1971). The second schema insouciantly ignores changes that are at least real enough to prompt Kastenbaum's crisis of explanation. On the constructionist model, all but the most debilitating negative symptoms will be discounted as the products of unfortunate socialization and cultural stereotypes. Moreover, the epistemological implications of both schemata are unacceptable. With the senility-script model, reasoning and interpretive adaptiveness are increasingly untrustworthy, even if no negative symptoms are evident. Deterioration is assumed to be inevitable and, if not evident, taken as masked by rationalization or coincidence and present in undetected discursive discontinuities and confusions. And with the construc- tionist model, called-for assessment of reasoning and interpretive adaptiveness in advanced age is precluded by refusal to allow its special need.

Our culture's stereotypic interpretive schemata for old age insure that too many aging individuals understand neither that their age-generated cognitive crises are interpretive, nor that the stereotypic "solutions" our culture offers are themselves interpretive. While such understanding would not change the factual situation, it would go some way toward enabling aging individuals to better cope with what they face. Most importantly, understanding of the interpretive nature of the crisis would enable individuals to appreciate that the crisis is an occasion for assessment and decision, not acquiescence, and that there is time for productive assessment and decision. It is crucial to understand that the crisis is a kind of prelude, not the occasion for acceptance that something has *already* occurred. The aging individual must appreciate that she can and has to decide how she will deal with old age, as opposed to simply acknowledging and accepting that old age has overtaken her. Adoption of a cultural stereotype is in effect abandonment of any possibility of controlling her old age—including the possibility of simply forgoing it. And the stereotypic schemata insure that even if the person I am calling "reflective" understands that her culture's stereotypes are operant in how she is seen and treated and perhaps in her own thinking, she faces a problem Hamlet did not face in his epistemological crisis. She must contend with the fact that just when she most needs productive interaction with others, those around her see and hear her through distorting filters which warp or even preclude the communicative interaction that alone can provide her with external standards for assessing her situation and prospects. If the response of others to the concerns expressed by the aging individual are only commiseration, condescension, empty reassurances, or quick changes of subject to "spare her feelings," the aging individual will be hopelessly isolated.

Reason Enough?

It will seem to many that what has been said thus far simply does not suffice to raise the question of preemptive suicide in a serious way. Suicide prompted only by fear of intellectual decline is at best reserved for romanticized cases where dedicated artists take their lives because of despondency about flagging creativity, or, as in the case of Virginia Woolf, because the very sensitivity that has made them artistically productive makes them unable to cope with depression or boredom. It will seem that most of the foregoing is too unyielding and that consideration of suicide is not warranted by what has been said about the imperilment of what is, after all, a fairly high level of intellectuality. Though a likely objection, the most compelling articulation of it I have encountered was voiced by Chris Beeman, the painter. Beeman sees my concern with the maintenance of intellectual identity as less the prizing of something possessed than a too-demanding requirement that certain intellectual standards always be met. That requirement supposedly discounts the value of other, if more passive, aspects of life. As a productive artist who had to deal with the debilitating consequences of mononucleosis, Beeman learned not to demand more of himself than is consistent with his somewhat reduced capacities. He came to understand how the desire to *be* something is sometimes a drive to *do* something. In his view, what I see as prompting thoughts of suicide should prompt only reassessment and a measure of resignation. He thinks the need to retain intellectuality, which I conceive as centrally constitutive of self, is only a desire to continue to meet self-imposed standards of performance. Beeman believes we should be prepared to acknowledge and tolerate some diminishment of intellectuality as decline in a less-than-self-defining performative aspect of our lives—and do so for the sake of what life might still offer, such as close relations with others. It is true that one can imagine oneself reaching a time in life when intellectual achievement, perceived as only one of the sorts of things we are capable of achieving, is forgone for the satisfactions of family life or companionship. I appreciate the point that the concern with intellectuality may have more to do with achievement than with the maintenance of a self-defining capability. I also realize life does have a great deal to offer that is of real value beyond the intellectual. The gist of my response to Beeman is that the validity of the consideration of preemptive suicide ultimately depends on what one values and what one is willing to bear. But it is important to meet Beeman's objection in a fuller way, because I suspect it would be pressed by most readers of this book. Meeting the objection is in part the burden of the rest of the book; nonetheless, I will here anticipate later discussion by saying a little about the notion of intellectuality operant in my thinking.

In this chapter the point has been to consider how preemptive suicide arises as an option for an aging individual. The way that option arises has been discussed here—and in the previous chapter—in terms of the endangerment of an individual's intellectuality. That endangerment has been portrayed as the most threatening aspect of aging. Recognition and anticipation of the risk of intellectual diminishment have been offered as sufficient to raise the question of whether one might not be better off dead than living with waning faculties. The objection to all this is basically that there is more to life than intellectuality, and that even a highly reflective person may enjoy a reasonably happy old age in the company of her family or friends in spite of serious intellectual diminishment and while retaining only the faintest memories of what she has lost. Higher-level thought and perspicacious self-reflection, it is argued, are not the highest values in human life, and their loss does not justify suicide. I admit to finding some difficulty in appreciating this objection. For one thing, I think there is a tendency for those who raise the objection to conceive of intellectuality too narrowly as a less-than-necessary capacity for problematically useful abstract thought. And there is an attendant tendency to think of self-reflection as intrusive self-consciousness—even as a Kierkegaardian bar to authenticity. I am not here assuming that intellectuality and self-reflection *so conceived* are of the highest value and that their threatened loss justifies abandonment of all other value. My point is that what is most central to our being is that we are self-aware reasoning entities. We not only reason in a means-to-ends fashion, we assess and reflect on what we do and what happens to us. We achieve an intentional (Edwards, 1967: 201–4) distance which enables us to be and act in the world as intelligent entities—as opposed to merely *reacting* to our environment as sentient and efficient but unreflective organisms. A time comes when a reflective person realizes or at least anticipates that she is beginning to lose the intentional distance that defines her as a self-consciously intelligent being. She then discerns or fears that her aging body can no longer support her previous mode of awareness—if only because its ailments immerse her ever more in her own workings. In my view this is enough reason for her to wonder if further life might not be best forgone to avoid the agony of experiencing even the beginnings of intellectual death in advance of physical extinction. Beeman sees the changes taking place as just that: changes. He does not accept that these changes are inherently disastrous as I do. Perhaps the best way to articulate the difference between Beeman and myself is to say that he can imagine acknowledging fundamental changes in himself—changes which the personal histories of millions strongly suggest are never for the better—with equanimity and hope of other still-attainable value. But to me those changes amount to the end of the being I am, even though they do not mark the end of me as a living organism.

The reflective person may acknowledge the beginning of fundamental change in herself with optimism—and, ironically, if deterioration moves apace she will never be disappointed. Or she might, more realistically, only hope there will be compensation for expected decline. But she may cast Yeats's cold eye on life and be willing to pass it by because her values and priorities are such that she does not want to continue living as, in effect, another person. She may not want to live on wholly immersed in whatever events constitute her life if unable to add to those events the reflective meaningfulness that raises them above what an animal may enjoy. If the reflective aging person takes the colder view, she will see rational preemptive suicide as her last fully deliberate act, as the last responsible act of a specific person whose existence is ending—ending because it is the fragile product of a delicate neurophysiological balance which is growing increasingly unstable. Nor should it be forgotten that the colder view of advanced age is not limited to age's intellectual aspect. The reflective person also understands that because of grosser physical changes she is reaching the end of her life as an autonomous individual; soon she will no longer be able to be and do largely as she chooses. Soon constraints on her will cease to be only social and moral and become personal in a way she may wholly reject. She will grow increasingly dependent on others, she will begin to lose control not only of her activities but over her own body, and she will be growingly plagued by chronic dysfunction, if not crippling maladies. And perhaps worst, she will face a future in which there can be no long-term improvement in her condition. When compared to the final stages of deterioration in advanced age, the earlier onset of intellectual precariousness is only a preamble. But *as* a preamble, it fortunately comes when the individual is still able to make hard decisions about her future. By the time deterioration has advanced to a point where it begins to hamper the individual, it is more than likely too late for those decisions to be made, if not because of a loss of power to make them, then likely because of a loss of power to enact them. The reflective individual faces a last choice on realizing that her existence as an intellectual entity has been jeopardized or is already being eroded by advanced age, and that eventually personal diminishment will destroy her well before physical death. The choice she must make is not so much whether to live or die; rather it is whether or not to allow a newly emerging but unreflective and powerless version of herself to continue living. She may make the hard decision that the emerging version of herself—intellectually crippled, socially powerless, and predisposed to illness—does not merit life.

3

SUICIDE AND RATIONALITY

The weariest and most loathed worldly life
  . . . is a paradise
To what we fear of death.
                    Shakespeare, *Measure for Measure*

Our culture's prevalent view, one with evident biological roots, is that life is the ultimate value; that life is worth preserving at all costs for its own sake. A more sophisticated but still uncompromising view is that as the precondition of all other values, life is to be preserved unless and until other values become irrevocably unattainable (Hook, 1988). In keeping with the view of life as the ultimate value, or at least as the condition of all other values, is the currently dominant conception of suicide as essentially pathological: "we now tend to treat suicide as the product of mental illness, or as a desperate dangerous 'cry for help' used by someone who does not really want to die" (Battin, 1982). It is true that the second of the foregoing views is now gaining acceptance, and that it tolerates consideration of suicide in cases of terminal illness and under similar circumstances where conditions effectively preclude the attainment of all other values. Nonetheless, death remains something to be considered as a voluntary option only in the most extreme circumstances. Even in cases where there is no hope of improvement of a terminal condition, expressed desire by the affected individual not to be kept alive by extreme measures is usually dismissed as insufficient to justify voluntary abandonment of life. In a recent right-to-die case the judge rejected a family's appeal to stop artificially sustaining the life of an elderly stroke-damaged relative. In doing so he dismissed the patient's own explicitly and repeatedly expressed wishes not to be kept alive by saying that her statements could not be "held to be clear and convincing proof of a general intent to decline . . . treatment once incompetency [set] in" (Chief Judge S. Wachtler, in Shipp, 1988: 36). There is an important point being made here about too-ready acceptance of a patient's remarks, but what is obvious is that even expressed willingness to abandon life in hopeless circumstances is simply not accepted at face value. The working assumption is that what is actually sought is not death but help, reassurance, and comfort. It is assumed that no one can literally want to die, regardless of their circumstances. To reject life-support treatment must be only to express horror at harsh realities. In the common view, voluntary death, much less self-inflicted death, is still not condoned unless prompted by *utter* hopelessness—and it is clearly contentious what counts as such. As we considered in a preliminary way in Chapter 1, suicide is perceived as justifiable only in those cases where the suicidist or potential suicidist was or is under extraordinary pressure of a maximally negative sort. Most people are quite unwilling to countenance cool, reflective suicide done because one decides not to endure a less than extreme but still punishing condition or judges it the most sensible thing to do *prior* to serious and diminishing deterioration. There is a strong conviction that self-inflicted death could never be merely the most sensible option, that it could never really be an option at all for anyone not in an extreme situation. Suicide is deemed to be a *driven* act, the outcome of maximum desperation or fatal confusion—or just possibly of consummate sacrifice: the laying down of one's life for one's friends, for moral principle, or because of religious or political commitment. While there are signs of change (see, e.g., editors' column, *The New Republic*, Nov. 27, 1989), present attitudes prevent an elderly potential suicidist from receiving the counsel and support necessary for the making of a sound suicidal decision.

The first step toward changing present attitudes is to identify and deal with the most basic reservations people have about suicide. Many of these reservations will be grounded in ethical and religious doctrines, but some are more fundamental in the sense of being conceptual or epistemic. The most fundamental reservation, manifest in the perception of suicide as pathological, is that suicide can never be rational. More specifically, and more relevant to my concern, a suicidist's preference of death over life in the absence of disastrous circumstances is seen as unthinkable without self-deception, bewilderment, or compulsion. The whole point of characterizing suicide as pathological is to explain all of its non-desperate instances as products of derangement. As we saw earlier, cases of self-inflicted death prompted by the most extreme and irremediable circumstances are often not deemed cases of suicide, precisely because in those cases it makes good sense to die and there is need to qualify the assumption that no one can rationally want to die. This common perception of suicide as pathological is articulated in various philosophical claims which try to say just how suicide is never a rational act, but the claims in question are rarely couched in adequately precise terms. As we saw in Chapter 1, the basic issue with respect to the rationality of suicide has to do with the coherence of preferring to die, but as we also saw, there are five other relevant senses in which suicide must be rational. More often than not the sense of rationality involved in claims about the nonrationality of suicide is merely assumed to be intuitively clear. This means that likely only one or another of the six senses of rationality considered here—coherency, utility, consistency (discursive, judgmental, and behavioral), and compatibility with values and interests—is actually addressed. One indication of the way many of the claims against the rationality of suicide fail to go to the heart of the matter is that these claims usually involve tacit or explicit redefinition of suicide so as to exclude nobly sacrificial self-inflicted death, as well as allow a certain leniency with respect to characterizing self-inflicted death as suicide in cases of terminal illness. What is meant, when self-inflicted death in a terminal condition is described as "not really suicide," is that the act precisely *was* rational because of the individual's circumstances. This juxtaposition of rational action and suicide as polar opposites is evident in the case in point I now want to consider. It is not my intention to enter into polemical discussion of the views of particular philosophers, but it is necessary to consider a paradigmatic attempt to establish the nonrational nature of suicide. I will mention individuals only as representative thinkers, and will sketch their theses rather than treating them as subjects for thorough exposition and debate.

The Lack-of-Contrast Argument

Among those who think suicide is never rational is John Donnelly, who contends that "we know (as an article of commonsensism) that suicide is not rational" (Donnelly, 1978: 89), and whose definition of suicide excludes self-inflicted death in terminal-illness cases and where the alternative is some otherwise inescapable gross moral wrong (Donnelly, 1978: 93). In Donnelly's definition the culturally most acceptable cases of self-inflicted death are conveniently removed from the category of what is described as "self-murder," and suicide is isolated as a special, nonrational sort of self-inflicted death. Donnelly's views on suicide are of interest less because they are particularly original or well-argued than because they serve as a good example of attempts to pin down the putative nonrational nature of suicide. Moreover, our question about the potential suicidist's understanding of the consequences of her act, and so of her ability to rationally opt for death, comes close to being addressed in the denial of the possibility that anyone can intelligibly evaluate being dead as desirable. The argument's point is that in order to rationally commit suicide, someone must be able to judge that being dead is *better* than being alive, and allegedly cannot do so because it is conceptually impossible to evaluatively contrast being dead or not existing with being alive or existing. While this is not quite a denial that one is able to sufficiently understand the annihilatory nature of death in order to knowingly prefer dying, the denial that one can intelligibly prefer being dead does approach rejection of the possibility of sufficient understanding, for what is denied is that anyone can have a coherent evaluatory basis on which to ground the preference to die. What the argument specifically rejects is the conceptual possibility of an evaluative *comparative* contrast between inconceivable nonexistence and experienced existence.

Briefly, the lack-of-contrast argument is that the decision and/or preference to die cannot follow as a consequence of sound deliberation because it is not possible, in that deliberation, to compare in an intelligibly evaluative way the state of being alive with the *non*-state of being dead. The argument's objective is to demonstrate the irrationality, or at least the arationality, of suicide by showing that the preference to die cannot have a rational basis. The potential suicidist can never prefer dying to continued life because she can never meaningfully evaluate *being dead* in her consideration of suicide. If she does prefer to die, it allegedly will always be because what she confusedly assesses as most desirable is not being *dead*, but rather some misconceived state of posthumous (continued) being. Her decision to die is not rational, then, because rooted in confusion.

The essential idea of the lack-of-contrast argument has a forceful initial plausibility, being that to contemplate suicide in a rational manner, the potential suicidist would have to weigh the supposedly manifest value of being alive—even in whatever punishing circumstances have prompted the consideration of suicide—against being dead or not existing. The trouble supposedly is that the latter alternative cannot be assigned a value because it is not any form of being, and attempting to assign it a value allegedly requires treating the unthinkable non-state of death as an assessable state (Donnelly, 1978: 96). Since being dead is not a very special kind of being, it cannot be compared in evaluative or any other terms to being alive. So instead of attempting to show that we cannot have Harman's "vivid awareness" or full understanding of the consequences of suicide, the lack-of-contrast argument tries to show that we cannot make an evaluative judgment about those consequences. The strong point of the lack-of-contrast argument is that rather than raising difficult questions about our capacities to conceive and understand something, it impugns the logical possibility of assigning a value to what one allegedly prefers in choosing to die. Since it is a non-state, being dead simply cannot be a proper object of preference. Nor can being dead then be a proper object of intention, since what is intended is at least in some broad sense always what is desired or preferred as the outcome of action. Contrary to Donnelly's view, my position is

that advanced age raises in a pressing way the question of
suicide as a rational alternative to the dissipation of personality
through loss of intellectuality and inevitable grievous loss of
autonomy, dignity, and even minimal personal comfort. I think
Hume is right in saying that "suicide may often be consistent
with interest and with our duty to our selves . . . " (Hume,
1963b: 595). However, for suicide to be a rational alternative
to demeaning old age, and for Hume to be right, we must
be able to rationally choose death over life at some point
in our lives. This means that the lack-of-contrast argument
must be answered. To do so I will show that the lack-of-
contrast argument appears to work only because it manufactures
a conveniently inconceivable intentional object for suicidal
deliberation, and substitutes that creation for the actual objective.

The Preference for Death

The basic issue is whether it is conceptually possible for someone to judge that death is preferable to a life which has or soon
will become burdensome and, moreover, which one would live
as an essentially different and diminished person. What this
comes to is that there must be a form of suicide which is a
rationally justifiable ending of one's own life after cool, well-
reasoned reflection and consultation. This sort of suicide must
be rational in that it is coherent for the individual concerned to
prefer to die and to have her own nonexistence as her intentional
objective. What makes matters more difficult for my purposes
is that the suicide which concerns me is not prompted by a
desperate physical or ethical dilemma, so cannot be one of
Donnelly's allowable exceptions. Instead it is prompted by the
realization that the quality of the life left to one is seriously
and irrevocably jeopardized by the inevitable consequences of
the sheer accumulation of years. Rational preemptive suicide in
advanced age is an act in line with Hume's belief that there is a
crucial duty to oneself to not allow the kind of diminishment of
self that general deterioration and certain chronic conditions can
bring about, that such diminishment of self warrants self-inflicted
death as much as appalling terminal illness or being forced to

irrevocably violate all of one's most deeply held convictions. What concerns me, then, is suicide as a rational act following on the compound realization that bearing diminishment for the sake of sheer survival is pointless, and that the time to take one's own life may be well before one is driven to it or becomes a candidate for euthanasia. I cannot ease the burden of proof of the coherency of preferring to die by making death attractive in contrast to desperate circumstances. The preference must be for death now because of anticipated, not actual or even imminent, developments. I am concerned with preemptive, not euthanatic suicide or suicide made necessary by an insurmountable moral threat. Donnelly's charge of the impossibility of preferring death therefore goes to the heart of my position.

To begin to answer the lack-of-contrast argument, two points about the definitionally allowed exceptions need to be mentioned. First, euthanatic suicide is of secondary philosophical importance because usually rational since its consideration and enactment occur in contexts which are of an overwhelmingly pressing and hopeless nature as well as extremely traumatic. Even those who most staunchly deny the rationality of suicide are inclined to see euthanatic suicide as a special case, and as not only rational but in fact advisable. Second, with respect to suicide prompted by moral considerations, I am not sure what to say. This fate-worse-than-death notion is, I suppose, realistic enough. It is not hard to imagine a person committing suicide because otherwise she would be forced to do something that goes against everything she has lived for and that is of value to her. And we can imagine that act, if performed, plaguing the agent for the rest of a life made horrible by guilt. But the question of the general rationality of suicide to avoid ethical compromise seems to me to presuppose firm conclusions about the nature of ethical rules and conflicts, and so is beyond the scope of my project. To return to the central point, adherents of the lack-of-contrast argument deny that it can ever be meaningful to judge that being dead is or will be *better* than being alive, for such a judgment by the potential suicidist, who is still alive, is about an admittedly inconceivable future non-state which cannot be contrasted with anything at all. Third-person judgments about suicide are equally lacking in contrast, given that the suicidist either no longer exists or will soon not exist. Since there simply is no subject to bear any ascriptions after the death of the suicidist, no judgment can be made to the effect that the subject is or will be better off dead than alive. The logical power of this position is that any claim that being dead is preferable to being alive must involve misconception of being dead as somehow a state of subjectivity opposable to the state of being a living subject.

I think the lack-of-contrast argument is wrong, but must acknowledge that it captures something which feels intuitively right, namely, that choosing to die seems somehow senseless if one believes that death is irreversible annihilation. The lines from Shakespeare at the beginning of this chapter effectively state the idea that however bad life may get, while one still lives life could come to be endurable, whereas choosing to die is an utterly irrevocable abandonment of all possibility. The underlying truth here is that in assessing whether she would be better off dead, someone just cannot know whether what suicide enables her to avoid will in fact prove intolerable or whether it might not be somehow alleviated by compensating values. But we do know that once dead we irreversibly cease to exist. It would seem, then, that choosing to die must at the very least always be a precipitous decision. Another way of saying this is that it looks as if there can never be a final moment when we can conclusively judge that it is better to die. The lack-of-contrast argument leaves us thinking that at least one way in which we lack "vivid awareness" of the consequences of suicide is that in trying to assess if death is preferable to continued life, we never manage to evaluate the real consequences of suicide. This is where the lack-of-contrast argument is closest to a denial of the possibility of the coherence of preferring to die, because we allegedly either confusedly contrast continued life with some impossible state of posthumous subjectivity, or simply fail to put a value on the non-state of being dead.

An Ethical Aside

The lack-of-contrast argument has clear ethical implications, in that if a rational decision cannot be made for suicide, then no ethical decision can properly be made for it. And if, as said in Chapter 1, suicide is always a matter of confused intentions, ethical prohibitions against it must be taken as effectively prohibitions against considering suicide. The prohibitions must be against risking envisagement of a course of action which cannot be rationally deliberated and carried out, so could not be ethically legitimized—but which could be psychologically facilitated by rationalization. The ethical injunction must be against putting oneself in a position where suicide might look desirable, and where its commission could then result from distorted deliberation. The cases that concern me, where suicide is considered in other than desperate situations, are even more suspect than those where desperate situations force consideration of suicide. It looks as if consideration of suicide in the absence of overwhelming threat must amount to flirtation with both the unethical and the incoherent. It seems, then, that coherency-injunctions and ethical-injunctions equally obstruct consideration of preemptive suicide. However, these injunctions are not of equal force. The ethical injunctions here borrow some of their force from the allegation that it is incoherent to value being dead more than being alive. And whatever other force they may have derives from presupposition of specific value systems, each of which is open to challenge. Nonetheless, precisely because I am not concerned with cases where extreme pressures may override ethical prohibitions against suicide, and am concerned with cases where personal discretion is greatest—and so where ethical prohibitions appear strongest—it is important to briefly clarify earlier remarks about how ethical issues are actually secondary to the present project. And it is important to do this in the context of the lack-of-contrast argument since, as indicated, some of the force of the ethical injunctions against suicide comes from conception of suicide as never rational.

Many will be impatient with extended discussion of the rationality of suicide, perhaps dismissing conceptual reservations and arguments about something that is plainly possible, and thinking that what is truly important is whether taking one's own life can be the ethically right thing to do. Jan Narveson is representative of those who feel that the ethical questions are paramount and that there are "two main moral issues regarding

suicide: first, whether suicide is morally permissible, . . . and
second, whether a person . . . has an obligation to intervene"
(Narveson, 1986: 104). Narveson does not ignore the question
of the rationality of suicide, as we will see in considering his
contribution to criteria for rational suicide, but like many others
he devotes his efforts primarily to the ethical issues. However,
I continue to maintain that it is actually a confusion to think
all the important questions about suicide are ethical in nature.
The primary question about suicide is whether we can properly
reason our way to the decision to die. Before the issue of taking
one's own life is an ethical one, it is an epistemological one, not in
some doctrinaire way, but because of the conceptually antecedent
question whether the central elements of suicidal deliberation
can be adequately understood, weighed, and pondered. Prior
to ethical prohibitions against taking one's own life there is the
requirement that doing so be a fully responsible and witting act.
If the decision to take one's own life turns out to be so counter
to our nature that it must always be a forced one, or so confused
that the agent does not really intend to die by her action, then as
we saw earlier, ethical prohibitions would simply be redundant
in the first sort of case, or at best relevant to the *consideration*
of suicide in the second sort of case. However important the
ethical questions, they must be accepted as secondary unless
it can be made reasonably clear that they directly affect the
rationality of suicide. For instance, I suppose it would be
possible to mount a Socratic argument that the evident ethical
wrongness of suicide precludes its being intelligibly held as an
object of intention because we cannot do wrong knowingly.

The Argument Again

To return to the matter most immediately at hand, it may
seem that the way to answer the lack-of-contrast argument is
to produce cases where it can be established that an actual or
anticipated condition is or will be wholly intolerable, and in
that way provide a real contrast between the respective values
of continuing to live and dying. It would appear that given
that contrast, a judgment could be rationally made to the effect

that annihilation is preferable to that otherwise inescapable and insufferable condition. But it is a hopeless project to attempt to establish a contrast between personal annihilation and some situation so threatening as to be known to make annihilation preferable. Not only can we not know beforehand whether some anticipated situation in fact will prove unendurable in itself, we could never predict with certainty that the situation might not be compensated for in some way—if only through a strengthening of our own tolerance. What would need to be established is that the anticipated situation would be unendurable in simply occurring, and that appears very difficult. It would seem that the best candidate for such a type of situation would be an ethical one where the actual survival of the agent would itself contravene some major principle: for instance, the agent surviving at the cost of hundreds of innocents dying. But not only has Donnelly exempted just such cases, at this point one enters a stage of philosophical inventiveness that begins to look unrelated to real life, for the need is to think up cases where no unexpected factors could possibly render an envisaged situation less than wholly unendurable. A more productive strategy against the lack-of-contrast argument is to clarify that *being* dead is not itself one of the considered options in suicidal deliberation, but rather is the *consequence* of a negative choice: of a refusal to accept something else. It may initially appear that this is an overly subtle distinction, but a little reflection shows it not to be so. The point of the lack-of-contrast argument is that being dead cannot be one of the possibilities assessed in suicidal deliberation. As the argument has it, we cannot assign the non-state of nonexistence a value without turning it into a misconceived state in order to relate its assigned value to that assigned the state of continued existence. But the alternatives considered are not being alive and being dead; they are enduring an actual or anticipated condition or not enduring it. Dying, ceasing to exist, is a consequence of the latter alternative, not itself what is valued and chosen in suicidal deliberation. The comparative evaluation, then, is of the relative values of bearing something or not bearing something, where not bearing it entails dying. Annihilation is the price paid for not bearing whatever prompts consideration of suicide. The crucial evaluative assessment in the consideration of suicide is not the impossible one of whether nonexistence is better or worse than existence in the feared circumstances, but rather the quite possible one of whether or not one is *willing* to endure those circumstances. The choice here is not between two states, much less between a state and a non-state. The choice is between what one will and will not endure. The non-state of being dead only comes in when the decision not to put up with something has been made *and* enacted. Prior to that death is present only as the inevitable but still future consequence of choosing one of two alternatives. Admittedly death is the most overwhelming consequence of choosing not to endure conditions which must be endured if one continues to live, but it is not itself the primary object of choice. The lack-of-contrast argument works only if the consideration of suicide is construed as a wrongheaded attempt to evaluate being dead against continued life. Once that is appreciated, the argument ceases to be a conceptual bar to suicide as a rational choice not to bear something—where the consequence of choosing not to bear it is personal annihilation.

In the next section I will consider more fully the correct evaluative contrast in the consideration of suicide. However, it must be admitted that the nature of the evaluative contrast can be clarified as I have done only on the assumption that we can fully understand that the consequence of suicide *is* personal annihilation, and therefore understand the result of choosing not to endure some actual or threatened condition by committing suicide. So even though the lack-of-contrast argument addresses a different point than whether it is coherent to prefer to die, namely, whether it is intelligible to prefer *being* dead, nonetheless it indirectly raises our fundamental issue. In answering the lack-of-contrast argument we have to accept as coherent the preference to avoid something *at the cost of dying*. We can proceed, then, on the tentative understanding that the lack-of-contrast argument can be shown to be misconceived so long as it is in fact coherent to prefer to die—not as preferring to be dead, but as preferring to pay the price of annihilation to avoid what one is unwilling to bear. What we have gained is that suicide cannot be shown to be arational or irrational merely by pointing out that being dead is a nonstate which defies evaluation and so cannot provide a basis for rational suicidal deliberation and choice.

Criteria for Rational Suicide

Something of what is needed to establish the rationality of suicide is captured by Jacques Choron, who explains that in connection with suicide, not only must there be "no psychiatric disorder" and the agent's reasoning be "in no way impaired," rationality further requires "that his motives would seem justifiable, or at least 'understandable,' by the majority of his contemporaries in the same culture or social group" (Choron, 1972: 96–97). Unfortunately Choron's remarks do not go deep enough, for the sense of rational which he attempts to explicate is less fundamental than that of whether it is coherent to prefer to die. Choron's emphasis is on the nonimpairment and particularly the accessibility of reasoning in suicidal deliberation. He clearly assumes that the potential suicidist can appreciate the nature and consequences of what she is considering. Nonetheless, Choron does contribute to the resolution of the basic issue by pointing out how crucial it is that the potential suicidist's reasoning be accessible to others. However, as Margaret Battin has pointed out, Choron is overly optimistic in thinking that most people in our culture would be prepared to understand a suicidist's reasoning, since suicide is generally seen as pathological (Battin, 1982). Aside from the question of whether a potential suicidist's reasoning is accessible and plausible in itself, there is the question of whether her peers will think it plausible and even recognize it as reasoning. Choron's instincts are right, but Battin is correct in her assessment of his optimism. To many, any proffered suicidal reasoning will look like so much rationalization. Nonetheless Choron's point is well taken. There must be what I described in Chapter 1 as a critical measure of universality in assessment of suicide as rational. We cannot allow the rationality of suicide to be mere consistency with an individual's values and preferences and let whatever her thoughts may be count as reasoning. The underlying point is that even though neither ahistorical nor "objective," standards for rationality and reasoning cannot be particular to individuals or groups. Even without embracing some sort of objectivism or ahistoricism, it can be acknowledged that the main point of judging something rational or otherwise is usually to override

idiosyncratic individual and group judgments made on the basis
of operant values and preferences. What must be said here is that
Choron's insistence on the accessibility of suicidal reasoning is
insightful and important, even though it cannot be made out as
clearly as we might wish. Basically his demand is that suicidal
reasoning, if conducted without impairment, must have *the same
force* for others as for the suicidist—though not necessarily the
same outcome.

Battin responds to the charge that suicide is not rational by
offering a set of criteria for rational suicide. These criteria fall
into two broad groups:

> The first three, ability to reason, realistic world view, and
> adequacy of information, are . . . the "nonimpairment" cri-
> teria. The final two, avoidance of harm and accordance with
> fundamental interests, are . . . the "satisfaction of interests"
> criteria . . . We typically speak of a decision as "ration-
> al" . . . if it is made in an unimpaired way; we also speak
> of a decision as "rational" . . . if it satisfies [the agent's]
> interests (Battin, 1982: 289).

While hers is the most satisfactory criterial treatment I have
found, unfortunately Battin does not go deep enough either. Like
Choron, she fails to address the basic point about the coherency
of preferring to die. Her first nonimpairment requirement, the
ability to reason, may look to be at least a gloss on the
coherency issue, but that is not the case. The first criterion is
actually a methodological one. What it says is that the potential
suicidist must be able to engage in rational deliberation which is
unimpaired by extraneous factors, such as disruptive emotional
motives or neurotic or pathological obsessiveness. And in
fact, the second and third nonimpairment criteria could be
considered only special cases of the first. That is, in order
to reason properly about suicide, a potential suicidist must
not have a radically unrealistic world view, such as believing
in posthumous existence, or lack relevant information, such as
about her actual physical condition. But Battin essentially

assumes the coherency of the antecedent preference to die and instead addresses the criterial question of whether suicidal deliberation and enactment can be rational behavior. Battin's second nonimpairment criterion, having a realistic world view, is perhaps as close as these criteria come to the coherency issue, insofar as we can say that those who reject the rationality of suicide maintain precisely that no one who prefers to die has a realistic world view, because no one who prefers to die fully understands—or really intends—the annihilatory consequences of suicide. Battin is not unaware of the coherency problem, but she sees the issue as a purely psychological one, saying that while death is clearly a certain consequence of suicide, still "this is precisely what a great many suicides do not accurately foresee . . . " (Battin, 1982: 299). She adds that this is not as bizarre as it may seem at first, because "Freud claims that this is true of all people, insofar as the human unconsciousness 'believes itself immortal' " (Battin, 1982: 299). As noted in Chapter 1, Freud's claim does not raise a purely psychological problem, for it has the serious cognitive implication noted earlier, namely, that if we are in fact incapable of believing in our own annihilation, then preferring to die cannot be coherent because the preference is never really for death but rather for some unconsciously anticipated state of posthumous existence, or simply is not a preference at all because there is no real belief that one will die. However, the possible existence of distorting unconscious beliefs is not by itself sufficient to preclude the rationality of suicide. It can be argued that whatever may be true at the unconscious level, it suffices that potential suicidists accept the finality of death at the conscious level. That is, it can be maintained that deep unconscious beliefs are beliefs only in a special sense and cannot be abstractly integrated into conscious deliberation for the purpose of evaluating the rationality and soundness of that deliberation. If unconscious beliefs were relevant to the assessment of reasoning, we could never draw any conclusions about it, if only because of our inability to inventory unconscious beliefs that might affect any instance of reasoning. In any case, we do reason effectively and validly about matters which, in being contrary to the evidence of our senses, must be assumed to generate any number of unconscious beliefs. For instance, we know that what we witness at dawn is the horizon dropping, not the sun rising, in spite of the fact that at some level we likely do not believe—in some sense—that the ground beneath us is turning and instead believe it to be the paradigm of unmoving stability. Nonetheless, we reason effectively about any number of matters having to do with the Earth's rotation. Moreover, our assessments of reasoning do allow for unconscious beliefs in this way: once we accept as sound some piece of reasoning relating to action, we reserve judgment until we see if what the individual concerned actually does is consistent with that reasoning. If it is not, we may conclude that some distorting belief likely was or became operant. In the case of successful suicide things are made more difficult by the fact that there is no subsequent behavior to observe and assess, but there usually will be adequate indications, for instance in suicide notes, whether the act was carried out in keeping with reasoning we find sound, or whether in the event the suicidist revealed an underlying belief in some sort of posthumous existence. As for intended suicide, the assessment of the possible role of distorting unconscious beliefs can be carried out through discussion with the potential suicidist. This is one of the reasons why it is imperative that an aging potential suicidist have access to open-minded, productive consultation.

But disbelief in one's own annihilation does not occur only at the unconscious level, and it is here that Battin's second or realistic-world-view criterion comes into its own. Religious beliefs complicate the issue of suicide. Many individuals would not understand their act of suicide as resulting in their own annihilation, but rather would see it as a transition to a doctrinally guaranteed afterlife. In fact, for those same many the consideration of suicide poses ethical problems largely because they fear harsh judgment on entering that afterlife. In Chapter 1 I said belief in an afterlife precludes the coherence of the preference to die. This is because if someone believes in an afterlife, then taking her life is not intentionally annihilating herself, even though it is *materially* doing so. It may be that belief in an afterlife is no more than the conscious manifestation of the unconscious inability to accept our mortality, but it would still be necessary either to disabuse people of their illusions if they are considering suicide or, what is more likely, to concede that most religious people—and those having some sort of secular belief in posthumous existence—are not capable of making a fully rational decision about ending their own lives. I simply do not know what else to say about someone who even half-believes that we survive death in some form or other. Anyone who believes we survive our own deaths seems to me to not have Battin's "realistic world view." I find the notion of an afterlife incomprehensible. While at one time I believed that after death we were judged and allocated to one or another realm, I do not now understand what it was I believed—or thought I believed—unless it was simply myself *not dying* in spite of envisioning a body supposedly my own ceasing to function and being buried. I cannot authentically attempt to factor into my present thinking about the rationality of suicide some elusive idea about posthumous survival, and in what follows I will put aside questions about the rationality of suicide conceived as only a transitional act. My justification for doing so is as follows. Suicide forced by unbearable circumstances is not of primary importance to my project simply because not the subject of investigation. Suicide conceived as only a radical change in mode of existence also is not of primary importance for the same reason. Nor is it incumbent on me to consider transitionally conceived suicide. The notion that we survive our own deaths is problematic enough that the onus is on those who accept it to establish reasonable grounds for believing that we survive physical death before demanding consideration of transitional suicide. Furthermore, even if there were some possibility that we survive our own death, given the lack of adequate evidence, suicide undertaken on the assumption that we do so would be irrational in the same sense that a hopeless wager is irrational. The point of Battin's second nonimpairment criterion is precisely that for an act of suicide to be rational, the potential suicidist must not be under any illusion about the consequences of her act—which is to say that she cannot rely on some ill-defined and unsupported belief that she will survive her own death. What is basically in question in our discussion is what Albert Camus perceptively maintained was the fundamental philosophical issue: *deliberately ceasing to exist* (Camus, 1955). Consideration of suicide and the rationality of suicide must be first about self-caused annihilation, for without compelling evidence of some form of survival, choosing to end one's life can be rationally deliberated only as opting for nonexistence.

Battin's third nonimpairment criterion, adequacy of information, is not of special importance in the present context. It has to do with a potential suicidist not being misinformed or ignorant, as in the case of someone taking her own life while thinking she has a terminal disease, when she in fact is suffering from a non-fatal ailment. Of considerably more interest and relevance are the satisfaction-of-interests criteria: avoidance of harm and congruence with fundamental interests. The point of most arguments against the rationality of suicide is that suicide is always the worst possible self-inflicted harm and is never in the interest of the potential suicidist. The suicidist allegedly does irremediable harm to herself, and so violates her own most basic interests. Suicide can be rational only if it is both in the interest of the suicidist and, while admittedly self-inflicted harm, is at least less harmful than allowing oneself to go on living. Battin makes the very sensible and pivotal point that in assessing whether one harms oneself in committing suicide to avoid something deemed unbearable, we have to look at "the amount of other experience permitted . . . and whether this other experience is of intrinsic value" (Battin, 1982: 312). For Battin the assessment of whether suicide is the greatest self-inflicted harm, and hence irreversibly against one's interests, is a matter of assessing the degree and persistence of the negative element to be borne in continuing to live, and whether its being borne is made worthwhile by "important experience during the pain-free intervals" (Battin, 1982: 312). By allowing relative weighting of interests against suffering in this way, Battin's position is contrary to the popular view that suicide must be the worst self-inflicted harm to one's interests and so can only be justified when one is in the position of in effect no longer having interests because of terminal illness or some other dire and hopeless predicament. In the popular view the preservation of life is held so absolute that it is assumed a duty incumbent on everyone without regard to whether it is one's own life or another's that is preserved. It is significant that the law allows interference with attempted suicide, which is precisely described as prevention of self-inflicted harm, as a universally available defense against any charges incurred in the process of that interference. A representative passage in *Criminal Law Defenses* tells us that "society has nearly as strong an intangible interest in thwarting suicide as it does in thwarting murder" (Robinson, 1984: 193). Another passage brushes away the potential suicidist's reasoned decision, saying the potential suicidist's personal autonomy to commit suicide is simply "dismissed" in law (Robinson, 1984: 193; compare Shipp, 1988).

What Battin is after in arguing as she does is basically the point I made earlier against the lack-of-contrast argument, namely, that the evaluative contrast central to suicidal deliberation is not between being alive and being dead, but between the relative merits of continuing to live under certain risks or punishing conditions, or avoiding those conditions and risks at the cost of ceasing to exist. The popular view is very close to that of the lack-of-contrast argument, in that it disallows anticipation and rejection of future distress to count as an evaluative contrast to the value of continuing to live, in effect precluding anything *in* life to be weighed against life itself. Against this, the satisfaction-of-interests criteria begin with judgments about whether the good in life outweighs the bad. And if the judgment is that the bad outweighs the good, the decision to commit suicide is a decision to avoid the bad by dying. This decision is not Donnelly's choice between a state and a reified non-state. It is an abandonment of the state in which bad outweighs good. Once this point is seen, arguments such as the lack-of-contrast one reduce to the assertion that we can never know that future distress will be unbearable, can never know that the bad in life will outweigh the good. But this assertion need not be contested here, because the issue of preemptive suicide is not about what one *can* bear. It is about what one is *willing* to bear. The claim that anticipated distress cannot justify suicide because we might grow more able to bear that distress is really all but irrelevant to the issue. Bearing personal diminishment is not surviving while courageously bearing distress; it is to be made into a lesser person whose thought and priorities are reduced to the most rudimentary and whose sensitivities are blunted, and in that sense it is to cease to exist as surely as by dying.

Rationality Again

Battin is as overly sanguine as Choron if she thinks that she has dealt with the question of the rationality of suicide—if that question includes the coherency of the preference to die—by providing the criteria she does. Even if the lack-of-contrast argument can be met, as a paradigm of arguments against the rationality of suicide, the question remains as to whether it is coherent to prefer personal annihilation in order to avoid what one is unwilling to bear. Both Battin and Choron seem to think that the core of the issue about suicide's rationality is unimpaired reasoning, and that the coherency-of-preference issue is either a matter of whether suicide can be shown to be in the potential suicidist's interests and consistent with her values, or a purely psychological question. Unfortunately, the criteria offered could be satisfied and it might still not be coherent to prefer to die. For instance, the Freudians may be right and any such preference, when being enacted, is always distorted by confusion about the outcome of the act of suicide or the nature of death. Freud insisted that "it is . . . impossible to imagine our own death . . . whenever we attempt to do so we . . . are in fact still present as spectators," and that "at bottom no one believes in his own death" (Freud, 1915: 289). That insistence continues to pose a problem in spite of what was said above about unconscious beliefs. The reason is that even though we may be able to block the claim that unconscious beliefs undermine suicidal deliberation and enactment, perhaps suicide is never rational because it is never in the event a fully intentional act. That is, it may be that what the suicidist *consciously* intends at the crucial moment in which she takes her own life is in fact never her own annihilation. Self-distraction of some sort or sudden hope of an afterlife could preclude the rationality of suicide as effectively as unconscious beliefs allegedly would. And if some such factor becomes operant, however sound and realistic the suicidist's deliberation may have been, it would then not be the actual basis for her act. What we have here is replacement of Freudian unconscious devices with behaviorally disruptive ones. We might conclude, then, that either people cannot rationally enact a well-reasoned decision to achieve their own annihilation, or, more likely, that we cannot establish that they can with enough confidence to say suicide can be rational. This conclusion would mean that any criteria for the rationality of suicide would never capture the act itself and would apply only to deliberation leading to it, which would make such criteria practically useless.

However, it can be maintained of *any* act that even though we are wholly convinced we deliberated properly and are performing the act wittingly, still the performance is the product of essentially causal factors. This is little more than psychological determinism. For one thing, the claim is unfalsifiable. As with psychological egoism—which postulates a self-serving motive as the ultimate impetus to every act—it would always be possible to conjure up a maverick motivating impulse or last-minute confusion to undermine the rationality of any act. Even if not deterministic, this possibility trades on the idea noted in Chapter 1 that there could be self-protective (e.g., self-deceptive) psychological reflexes comparable to physiological ones. To deflect this psychological objection we must require that *specific* reasons be given for doubts about the fully knowing and deliberate nature of preemptive suicide. As we earlier required that there be specific indications an unconscious belief distorted someone's suicidal deliberation, we must put the burden on the skeptic and require specific reasons for impugning the complete wittingness of preemptive suicidal enactment. If general doubt forced us to conclude that when all the relevant deliberative considerations have been taken into account, preemptive suicide could still be a result of some unspecified and postulated factor bearing no relation to deliberation, it would mean we could never understand someone's suicide by following or reconstructing her deliberation. What Choron appeals to when he speaks of a suicidist's peers' understanding of her reasoning has to be more than that we could successfully reconstruct the deliberation carried out by the suicidist but still fail to grasp the elusive deciding factor that made her enact the conclusion to that deliberation. We cannot allow mysterious "clinchers" distinct from what would then amount to deliberative window-dressing. Whether or not technically defeated, the force of the lack-of-contrast argument would remain intact if dying can be entertained as an alternative only in what turns out to be rational deliberation incompletely or even wholly unrelated to the actual act of suicide. We have to resist the general impugning of our ability to act intentionally and on the basis of reasons, even in so final a matter as taking our own life. And what enables that resistance is that the alternative is not only to admit that suicide cannot be judged to be rational, but to grant that *no* act can be judged to be rational.

Concern with enigmatic deciding factors and deep-seated rejections of mortality amounts to cognizance that in dealing with complex human behavior, we can never be conclusively sure of exactly what elements determine a decision or action taken. In most cases it is not very important to be able to arrive at firm and precise conclusions about the motivation of behavior, but if the issue is the rationality of deliberately bringing about one's own annihilation, there can be no room for *general* doubt about the connection between suicidal deliberation and action. This is where we most clearly see the importance of our primary question, because if it can be concluded that it is in principle coherent to prefer to die, then when someone chooses to die after apparently cogent deliberation and informed decision, we can require that doubts be articulated in terms of specific reasons to suspect the rationality of the particular suicide. In this way we can restrict the general doubt about the connection between rational suicidal deliberation and action to empirical issues about particular cases. We can then reject the idea that suicidal deliberation and the actual taking of one's own life are too tenuously connected, or may be too easily disjoined by psychological devices or unconscious beliefs, to allow the rationality of the deliberation to characterize the enactment of its conclusion. The requirement for specificity in challenges to the rationality of suicide prevents the relegation of the sort of criteria Battin and Choron offer to some never-never land of hopeless abstraction.

Requiring specific reasons for doubting the rationality of criterially sanctioned suicide seems to be an effective complement to the application of criteria testing the rationality of suicide. It looks, then, as if satisfaction of the criteria for rational suicide actually may resolve the coherency issue with which I began. It may do so by exhausting that issue of content. In light of what has been said, it does seem empty to say that even when the rationality criteria are satisfied there may still be lack of adequate understanding of the annihilatory consequences of suicide. This is especially so once we block the introduction of unconscious deliberation-distorting beliefs or mysterious motivating impulses, discontinuities, or befuddlement in the actual enactment of a suicidal decision. To insist that there may still not be the requisite "vivid awareness" would seem to either beg the question or to fail to understand what has been said. To proceed, then, we should pursue the criterial approach to the issue of rationality of suicide, assessing how it deals with each of the various senses of "rational" we considered in Chapter 1. And we will put aside the coherency-of-preference sense for the moment, since it could turn out to be redundant. It may be that those senses leave little or nothing to constitute what I described as the most fundamental sense of "rational" applicable to suicide. In other words, it may suffice to show that suicide is the most utile course of action, that it is decided on after sound reasoning, that it would be chosen and enacted in various similar circumstances, that it is consistent with the agent's values, and that it is consistent with the agent's interests. Narveson agrees with this general view, offering a usefully succinct discussion of at least a major aspect of the rationality of suicide. He considers the rationality of suicide mainly in terms of values, saying that explaining "what it means to have rational desires and values is not easy; but negatively, we can say that they pass the most basic tests of rationality if they are not founded on beliefs that are . . . false or illusory" (Narveson, 1986: 105). Given that the beliefs grounding the agent's values are not false, and that the agent's actions are well calculated to attain her ends and realize her values, what remains with respect to suicide is, "so far as rationality is concerned, a matter of whether that action is prescribed . . . [by] one's values" (Narveson, 1986: 106). In Narveson's view, "to see whether suicide could ever be rational . . . we have only to ask whether it could be recommended by a scheme of [sound] values" (Narveson, 1986: 106). Narveson's view, then, is that if an agent takes her life because well-grounded values "recommend" that in certain circumstances it is better to die than continue living, and she acts in an effective manner without impairment or distortion of reasoning, her suicide is rational. The well-groundedness of values is here made to bear the major weight of the rationality of ensuing deliberation and behavior. And because of this emphasis on values, Narveson's approach fits well with Choron's requirement that a suicidist's peers understand her reasoning and motivation. That understanding cannot be only cool intellectual reconstruction of a suicidist's reasoning. It must incorporate shared or at least appreciated values into the assessment of her deliberation and act. Like Choron, Narveson makes the reasoning and implementation of whatever action the values "recommend" essentially secondary. But again like Choron, Narveson has little to say about the suicidist's interests, which is why Battin's criteria are both more satisfactory in themselves and necessary complements to Choron's and Narveson's.

What we have, then, is the possibility of satisfying Choron's, Battin's, and Narveson's requirements in the following way: We would first consider and supposedly understand the potential suicidist's motivation and reasoning, feeling at least some of their force (Choron). We would then judge her suicidal deliberation sound (or otherwise) in the sense of meeting established standards of discursive reasoning and being unimpaired by error (Narveson), by neurotic or pathological factors (Choron), or by unrealistic notions or ignorance of relevant facts (Battin). We would next judge the rationality of the potential suicidist's values in terms of their not being based on false beliefs (Narveson), and establish that those values prescribe or at least allow suicide in the relevant circumstances (Narveson, Battin). We would then have to work a bit harder at establishing that suicide best serves the agent and does not harm her more than continuing to live would do (Battin). With respect to the other senses of rationality which I listed, we could take it that if suicide best serves the agent's interests, it will be the most utile course of action, and that if her reasoning is sound, anyone else in the same circumstances and having the same values would reach the same decision, as would the agent herself at another time. We seem to arrive at a point, then, where it looks as if all we have left to do is the detail work of showing particular suicides consistent with particular agents' interests and values. It is now reasonable to ask what more one could want with respect to establishing the rationality of suicide. Specifically, we must ask if there can be anything left to our primary worry that it might not be coherent to prefer to die.

An Unanswered Question?

Battin, Choron, and Narveson call our attention to a number of complementary elements integral to—and perhaps sufficient for—the rationality of suicide: nonimpairment of reasoning, satisfaction of interests, peer understanding, the well-groundedness of operant values, the consistency of suicide with those values, and the consistency of suicide with the individual's interests. It would seem that if these elements are present, along with the elements of utility and consistency of judgment and behavior—both of which seem to be entailed by the others—suicide must be rational. All of this appears to leave no room for us to still ask whether the potential suicidist can coherently prefer to die in the sense of whether one can knowingly prefer annihilation to continued existence and intentionally enact that preference. Surely the only question left is what we earlier relegated to secondary status, namely, the purely psychological question of whether particular individuals are capable of actually taking their lives while fully understanding that they are thereby annihilating themselves—and that is not a matter we can resolve with general arguments. So it does look as if all I need to do is show in a detailed way how suicide can be prescribed by certain values, how suicide can be consistent with the suicidist's interests, and—with respect to my special concern—how suicide can be consistent with interests when the potential suicidist's circumstances are not desperate. Still, my sense is that reservations remain. The question with which I began, about the coherence of preferring personal annihilation with Harman's "vivid awareness" of what that means, seems to persist. The trouble is that the criterial approach appears to carry insufficient conviction when what we are assessing is self-inflicted death. There does seem to be reason to think that in spite of the satisfaction of criteria such as Battin's, Choron's, and Narveson's, suicide may not be rational. Donnelly's easy talk of the "commonsensism" of suicide's nonrational nature is not just a silly mistake. Consider the case of a Japanese general committing *sepuku* (*hara kiri*) at the end of the Second World War on learning that Japan has been defeated, and rightly judging that his own failures contributed to that defeat. I think this case very likely would meet the various rationality criteria. (In spite of not being concerned with purely implemental matters, I will stipulate that the general, as an enlightened individual, forgoes the traditional but needlessly excruciating disembowelment procedure and simply puts a bullet through his head.) Assuming the reviewed criteria are met, could we, with respect to a case like the general's, still raise the question of the coherency of the preference to die? Is there anything left over that is not dealt with by the various criteria provided by Battin, Choron, and Narveson? I think we can still ask that question and that there is something left over. In the next two chapters I shall say how and what.

4

A QUESTION OF BALANCE

I hear only slow death preached, and patience with everything "earthly."

Nietzsche, *Zarathustra*

As I warned early on, repetition is the cost of clarity when dealing with a question as complex as the rationality of preemptive
suicide. For the sake of clarity, I will briefly recapitulate the
argument so far—adding one or two clarifications. In Chapter
1 I distinguished various senses in which suicide may be said
to be rational, focusing on the most fundamental, namely, that
in which suicide is rational only if—minimally—it is coherent to
prefer death to life knowing and fully understanding that death
is personal annihilation. The basic question, then, is whether
suicide can be rational in the sense of it being intelligible
to assess the cessation of existence as preferable to continued
living. But as we saw, there are a number of other senses of
"rational" to consider: the sense in which suicide is the most utile
alternative; the sense having to do with discursive consistency
in the suicidist's reasoning and deliberation; the sense having
to do with judgmental and behavioral consistency with respect
to similar cases; the sense covering the consistency of suicide
with agent-values; and the sense covering the consistency of
suicide with agent-interests. In Chapter 2 we considered how
the assessment that life is quickly ceasing to be worth living may
be prompted by conditions inherent to advanced age. Putting
aside questions of terminal illness and the like, we saw that

a reflective person may come to judge that her very survival to an advanced age has seriously jeopardized her continued survival as the reflective person she is and values being, thus threatening to diminish her in ways she is unwilling to risk for the sake of a few more years of life. In Chapter 3 I considered a paradigmatic argument against the rationality of suicide, namely, that suicide cannot be rational because being dead cannot be assessed intelligibly as preferable to being alive. We found that—as this formulation suggests—the argument relies on a confused characterization of what is assessed. In dealing with the claim that suicide is never rational, I reviewed a number of criteria which their various exponents believe, when satisfied, establish the rationality of suicide. However, reservations persisted as to whether satisfaction of the sort of criteria proposed could suffice to show suicide rational, especially in the fundamental sense of it being coherent to prefer to die.

Note that while couched in terms of living and not living, the discussion throughout has been basically about the continuation or cessation of *awareness* or of existence as a subject of experience. This is by no means always recognized to be the case. The margin for fatal confusion in the consideration of suicide is provided precisely by the way some potential suicidists erroneously distinguish between continued *life* and continued *awareness*. As Battin points out, in cases of pathological suicide of various sorts, the suicidist anticipates some kind of posthumous awareness in which she experiences, for example, the satisfaction of seeing loved ones regret her death (Battin, 1982). The facility with which this tragic confusion occurs is no doubt due in large part to our religious tradition, which doctrinally distinguishes between our "earthly" life, which may end, and our essential subjectivity, which supposedly will not end. Admittedly this religiously grounded confusion may be only a manifestation of our putative unconscious inability to accept our own mortality, but whatever its source, it is a fact that many potential suicidists deliberate only about the cessation of their "earthly" life, and not about the total eradication of their awareness. Nor is it only religion which fosters the foregoing confusion. Probably the majority of philosophers since Plato have at least accepted the possibility of continued awareness or subject-existence after "earthly" life. Even so thoroughgoing a materialist as D. M. Armstrong insists—and admittedly correctly—that continued existence as an aware subject after the death of the body is not logically impossible (Armstrong, 1968). But beyond this correct though minimal concession, there is a very strong tradition in the history of philosophy of actively arguing for the survival of a soul. However, as we saw in the last chapter, the issue of suicide allows no margins for mere logical possibility or problematic argumentation: it is about personal annihilation. Even allowing the logical possibility that we may survive our physical deaths in some form or other, the matter of the rationality of suicide must be considered in the most stringent terms: total cessation of existence as subjects. There is no room in our discussion for religious, philosophical, or romantic aspirations or illusions. Beyond faith and arcane arguments, we have no independent evidence that we survive death, and to contemplate suicide in the hope that we might is to allow our values a seriously disproportionate role in the reaching of a suicidal decision.

As should be evident from the discussion in Chapter 3, philosophers mainly address the rationality of suicide in terms of the satisfaction of various criteria for rationality, accepting that if suicidal deliberation is shown to be rational, there is nothing significantly at issue about the rationality of the act of suicide. Battin thinks that the rationality of suicide is capable of being dealt with "as a compound issue: can suicide be chosen in a rational way, and can it be the rational thing for a particular person to do?" (Battin, 1982: 289). And initially this looks to be enough. According to views like Battin's, Choron's, and Narveson's, it is possible to check for crucial features of suicidal deliberation, such as unimpaired reasoning and consistency with the agent's interests and values. The implication is, of course, that we can both define and identify such reasoning and consistency. Unfortunately, it would be an ill-advised epistemological move to articulate our reservations in terms which challenge our ability to define proper reasoning and consistency of behavior with values. As Narveson points out, we can produce adequate accounts of reasoning and consistency (Narveson, 1986: 105). But more important, to challenge our ability to define and recognize sound reasoning and consistency in the present context would be to immediately go beyond the issue of suicide to the broader and even murkier issue of human rationality and its standards. I have attempted that elsewhere, but have no need to do so here (Prado, 1987). In any case, Narveson is right; we can make do with definitions such as he offers. And as I stipulated in Chapter 1, the present discussion is geared to currently accepted standards of rationality. The problems with the criterial approach have less to do with standards and their application than with the fact that the criteria proffered by Battin, Choron, and Narveson largely assume the coherency of an *antecedent* preference to die, as well as that the rationality of suicidal deliberation carries over to its enactment. Certainly with respect to our basic question, it is fairly obvious that Battin's articulation of the issue, for instance, presupposes that suicide has arisen as a *legitimate* option and so as a coherent potential preference. And I have found in the literature only the most cursory treatment of the question whether rational suicidal deliberation insures rational commission of suicide. But my coherency question is admittedly an elusive one, and as we saw, easily confused with the psychological one of whether a particular suicide is rational or is made otherwise by unconscious beliefs, confusion, or other distorting factors. As suggested at the end of the last chapter, given that elusiveness, if it is true that the various criteria proposed are satisfied, it is at least unclear and problematic what more one might realistically expect to learn about the rationality of suicide. Battin and Choron and Narveson might well ask what more one could want.

The foregoing brings us to where we left off in Chapter 3: trying to pin down the nature of our reservations. And perhaps the articulation which best captures continuing unease about the coherency of preferring to die is that, given the finality of suicide, we wonder whether it can in fact ever be *reasonable* to take one's own life. The point here has to do with the difference between something's being *rational*, and its being *reasonable*. Though I will mainly use the more common rational/reasonable, the difference can be equally well marked by speaking of "thin" and "thick" senses of rationality. The difference in question is between rationality in the technical or abstract sense which governs consistency of premises, the drawing of inferences, and means-to-ends utility, and what people ordinarily mean by "rational" or "reasonable" or even "logical," namely, thought or action judged technically rational but also qualified and enhanced by considerations of circumstance, natural limitations, desirability of objectives, and value. Something can be strictly rational in the sense that a valid inference is rational, or it can be rational (i.e., reasonable) in the sense that given a particular context, operant values, and objectives, a decision or course of action is both in keeping with abstract rationality and well-advised and appropriate in the circumstances. The difference is analogous to that between the "letter" and the "spirit" of the law, which emerges when something that is strictly legal is nonetheless not permissible because of contextual considerations, consequences not foreseen by the framers of the particular law, or practices no longer tolerated by society.

Shakespeare again provides an apt fictive example: expecting payment of a contracted-for pound of flesh may be strictly legal and technically rational—in the "thin" sense and given a lawful contract—but it is hardly permissible or reasonable. Our reservations about criterially sanctioned suicide, then, might be put in terms of whether it is *reasonable* to avail oneself of a technically rational option, if doing so is the giving up of one's very life. This reservation simply reflects realization of the finality of suicide and the vast difference between something's being intellectually warranted and the hard reality of a specific individual's death. And however difficult the grounds for this reservation are to articulate clearly, they seem to be important. The reservation could arise forcibly in *every* case of suicide, thereby in effect repudiating avowals about the rationality of suicide. What is clear is that the logical space of the reservation is the application of the abstract judgment of the rationality of suicide to particular cases, and that a major factor prompting the reservation is the finality of the considered action. Putting the point in Battin's terms, the reservation has to do with whether suicide is rational—in the "thick" sense—for particular individuals. And the reservation amounts to wondering whether suicide, even though judged rational in the "thin" sense, is *ever* the right thing for *any* individual actually to do. The main focus in this chapter, then, must be the reasonableness of choosing wholly irrevocable annihilation because continued life is expected to involve conditions which one is not willing to risk, much less tolerate.

The first thing to do in proceeding is to pull together the various senses of "rational" we have considered, as well as the various criteria outlined in Chapter 3. By simplifying the list of relevant senses somewhat and combining and reformulating the several conditions for rational suicide, I can better clarify what can and cannot be dealt with, in determining whether suicide is rational, by articulating and applying criteria. In the balance of this chapter I shall describe and consider a case in point wherein the rationality criteria are putatively satisfied but which prompts productive reflection on the interplay between the elements the criteria test. The objective is to throw into sharper relief what—if anything—might be missed by the sort of criteria considered.

Re-assembling Senses and Criteria

Aside from the sense having to do with the coherency of preferring to die, the other senses of "rational" discussed so far have to do with utility and with consistency of various sorts: the consistency of suicidal deliberation with accepted canons of discursive thought as well as its internal consistency, the consistency of suicide with the agent's interests, the consistency of suicide with the agent's values, and the consistency of suicidal deliberation and action in similar circumstances. (In Chapter 1 we put aside the sense having to do with the means-to-ends rationality of suicide, which deals only with its most effective and least painful implementation.) But we need not continue to work with all of these senses of "rational." As suggested in the last chapter, if suicide does best serve an agent's interests and values, it will thereby be the most utile course of action for that agent. So long as we do not need to involve consequences to others, we can take it that the utility requirement is satisfied when suicide coincides with interests and values. As for the consistency of judgment and behavior in similar cases, here again we can take this requirement as met if the suicidal deliberation is sound and unimpaired. That is, we can assume that rationality is in some sense singular, and that if suicidal deliberation and enactment are rational in a given case, the decision reached and action taken will be the same in similar circumstances where the same values and interests are operant. We then can work with just three senses of "rational," those having to do with consistency with standards of discursive thought, with values, and with interests. These senses are satisfactorily, if somewhat diffusely, caught by the nonimpairment criteria provided by Battin and Choron, the accessibility criterion provided by Choron, the satisfaction-of-interests criterion provided by Battin, and the well-grounded-values criterion provided by Narveson. (It should be noted in passing that while these various criteria are productively articulated by the three thinkers mentioned, they are not unique to them. The criteria are representative articulations of the conditions usually set for rational suicide, and discussion of which constitutes the bulk of philosophical debate about the rationality of suicide.)

To proceed, I shall rephrase and condense the various criteria for the sake of clarity and effectiveness by amalgamating them into a tentative working definition of rational suicide as follows: Suicide is rational if suicide

1. follows on deliberation consistent with accepted canons of discursive thought and which is unimpaired by errors of reasoning, lack of relevant information, false beliefs, and/or compulsion;
2. is based on reasoning and interpretation of values accessible to others than the potential suicidist;
3. is prescribed by or at least consistent with the agent's operant, well-grounded values;
4. is in the interests of the agent, not harming the agent more than continuing to live would do.

For the sake of easy reference I shall call the first condition the "nonimpairment" criterion, as it rules out the distortion of reasoning by negative cognitive or psychological factors. The second condition I shall label the "accessibility" criterion, as it requires the cognitive publicity of the putatively unimpaired reasoning. The third condition I shall designate the "values" criterion, as it requires that suicide be dictated by what is prized, where what is prized is itself rational in the sense of not being based on false beliefs. And the fourth condition I shall dub the "interests" criterion, as it requires that suicide be to the agent's advantage and not be self-inflicted harm of a sort worse than its alternatives. The nonimpairment and accessibility criteria are basically procedural or methodological criteria, and assume the coherence of suicide as an option. Given that suicide has arisen as an option, they test if its consideration proceeds according to correct principles of reasoning and is not overly influenced or distorted by emotional and psychological factors. They also test whether that consideration can be followed and appreciated, if not accepted or endorsed, by others. The nonimpairment and accessibility criteria tend to reduce to the same practical test, for the force of saying that the potential suicidist's reasoning must be accessible to others is that it must be basically sound in order to be accepted by us *as* reasoning. Whatever else we may want to say about the standards for sound reasoning, they must be general: we must be able to see how the potential suicidist's reasoning progresses discursively and would apply to anyone in the same circumstances. The requirement that deliberation about suicide be accessible is a preclusion of discursive idiosyncrasy. We are not prepared to consider suicide rational if we cannot follow both how the potential suicidist herself moves from perception of some situation to the decision to take her own life, and how anyone else with her values and faced with her difficulties would go through the same progression. (The latter is the force of the consistency of judgment and behavior sense of "rational.") The values and interests criteria test whether an agent's values do or can sanction her self-inflicted death, and whether an agent's interests can intelligibly be said to be served by her self-inflicted annihilation. The values criterion also in effect tests whether any values requiring or prohibiting suicide are themselves rational.

As soon as we distinguish between the values and interests criteria we realize that there will be times when an agent's values and interests are at odds, and where her values color perception of her interests. As suggested earlier, there is a complicating dynamic factor generated by the possible opposition of an agent's values and interests, a factor that is highlighted by need for separate values and interests criteria. The question we face here is whether suicide, in being consistent with the potential suicidist's values, might not be at odds with her interests, and vice versa. The criteria are not independently satisfiable, since assessment of what is consistent with the potential suicidist's values must involve consideration of her interests, and assessment of what is consistent with her interests will be influenced by what she values. Whereas the nonimpairment and accessibility criteria, in being mainly procedural, are reasonably straightforward in application, the values and interests criteria have to do not only with the consistency of suicide with the potential suicidist's values and interests, but with what we can best describe as a proper balance in that dual consistency. The dynamic interrelations among values and interests are such that values and interests are to an extent mutually determining. The intertwined roles of values and interests even complicate the application of the nonimpairment and accessibility criteria, just to the extent that we may have difficulty in isolating the cognitive or procedural factors in the deliberation of suicide because of how values, and to a lesser extent interests, color perception and evaluation in reasoning. The basic point here is that if an individual values something enough, say personal honor, her interests will accommodate greater sacrifice—even of her life—because frustration of deeply rooted priorities or denial of what is highly prized may devalue the life her interests protect. Again, if it is in an individual's interests to live a long life, then the value she puts on personal honor may have to be lessened if honor's demands threaten her life in an unwarranted way. But these remarks are obviously too indefinite; to properly explore the dynamic interrelations among the potential suicidist's values and interests, as well as to more fully explore the criterial approach, we need to consider a case in point.

The Case of the General

Allow for the purpose of discussion that the Japanese general introduced in the last chapter is a proud soldier thoroughly committed to the samurai tradition of his culture. He coolly assesses his failures as an officer, rejects the possibility of a life continued in personal shame and dishonor, as well as one lived in a defeated nation, and decides he should end his life as prescribed by his code—though as specified earlier, he sensibly opts for a bullet over the ritual sword. The general's suicide satisfies the first or nonimpairment criterion: given his premises, his reasoning is sound and is unimpaired by psychological factors (he is not, for instance, morbidly depressed), lack of information (nothing has changed the situation), false beliefs (his failures as a general were significant), nor an unrealistic world-view (he holds no beliefs in divine emperors or a warriors' heaven). The second or accessibility criterion is also satisfied: the general's suicide is based on reasoning and an interpretation of values that is accessible to others—in fact his subordinates not only understand his decision, they admire it, they stand ready to participate in his (amended) *sepuku*, and may follow his example. The general's reasoning is also available to us, even though we are cultural outsiders. Despite our Christian culture's negative view of suicide, our pre-Christian history contains numerous examples of honorable suicide: Aegeus, Kleombrotus, Charondas, Lycurgus, Lucretius, Socrates, Demosthenes, Cato, Zeno, Seneca, Marcellinus, Brutus, and—rather marginally within our culture—Boadicea, Hannibal, and the hundreds at Masada. (Note that Christian martyrdom does not count as suicide, as it is always passive and at the hands of others.) We may, of course, reject the general's values and his assessment of his situation, but we would only be emphasizing that rejection if we claimed not to understand his reasoning.

So far, perhaps so good. Admittedly a number of things are being glossed over, but the example cannot be dismissed as obviously confused and does provide a plausible instance of the satisfaction of the nonimpairment and accessibility criteria. We might well agree here with Battin's point that in "the absence of any compelling evidence to the contrary," we have to accept that someone may choose suicide "on the basis of reasoning which is by all usual standards adequate" (Battin, 1982: 301). Nor is she suggesting that there are *unusual* standards to be considered. The point is that all the reasoning standards available to us appear capable of being met in some cases of suicidal deliberation. In the general's case, though we have excluded error and ignorance by hypothesis and stipulated proper reasoning, the point is that the example is fully intelligible as far as it goes. We come, then, to the two tougher conditions that must be met, those delineated by the values and interests criteria. (Having temporarily set aside the question of the coherency of the preference to die, we can take that preference as given in the general's case: in full knowledge of the consequences, and on the basis of his samurai code, he coherently prefers death to dishonorable life.)

In considering our case in point, the emphasis must be on the values criterion for two reasons. The somewhat more important reason is that in the cases which interest me—the taking of one's own life in less than desperate circumstances—suicide is prompted more by value considerations than interest considerations. The reflective aging individual does not consider preemptive suicide because she has a terminal illness or a moral dilemma which threatens her interests, but because she sees advanced age as eroding what she most prizes: her intellectuality and autonomy. There is a clear sense in which she is considering her interests, of course, but her primary motivation is what she values in being the person she is. The general's case is similar because his suicide is prompted by the value he puts on personal honor, not by illness or pressure of a similar sort. The second reason for focusing on values is that the values criterion plays a more central role in our culture than the interests one in determining the rationality of suicide. Our present cultural values insure that almost invariably interests are subordinable to values. There is a strong tendency to read "interests" as personal, and "values" as communal. We applaud the sacrifice of personal interests for communal values, and condemn the reverse. Our culture teaches that we should be prepared to sacrifice our interests for our values, as in patriotic sacrifice of our lives. "Greater love hath no man than he lay down his life for his friends" is thought to capture one of the noblest of human capacities. Putting one's interests ahead of one's values is thought to be one of our basest tendencies. We learn to view the sacrifice of values for interests as cynical, selfish, or immoral.

Having established that the general's reasoning meets the nonimpairment and accessibility criteria, the first question to ask is if the set of values operant in the general's case, the "samurai code" for brevity, is itself rational. I have factored out problematic elements from our case in point, such as religiously based illusions about an afterlife, and produced a thoroughly realistic exemplary general whose adherence to his samurai code is based purely on conceptions of personal honor and social obligation, and has nothing to do with notions of immortality or duties owed god-emperors. But my stipulations apply only to the general. The question now is about the rationality of the general's values. Would Narveson accept the samurai code as rational? Assuming, as I am doing throughout this chapter, that the general's preference to die is coherent, can he legitimately prefer to die, and can he reason properly about taking his own life, on the basis of the samurai code? Or does something about that code undermine the rationality of the suicide it prescribes? With respect to Narveson's idea that values are rational if not based on false beliefs, the relevant sort of foundational false belief would be if, for example, the samurai code held that the reason dishonored warriors must commit *sepuku* is to attain a Japanese version of Valhalla, and so conceived of suicide as transitional in the sense considered in Chapters 1 and 3. But our general accepts no such nonsense. If there is talk of losing his place in some warriors' heaven, he interprets it as meaning that he would live and be remembered as a shameful example of someone who put his own interests over his duties; if there is talk of his gaining a warriors' heaven, he interprets it as achievement of posthumous recognition of his courage and integrity. Our general's suicidal deliberation is carried out in terms of personal honor and social obligations. He does not allow mythical trappings to obscure either his thinking or the nobility of his code. (Consider this parallel: we may think that celebrating Christmas to ritualistically reinforce familial togetherness is an excellent practice, and continue to think so long after we stop believing in the Christ-child or Santa Claus.)

What quickly becomes evident is that the real focus of the requirement that values not involve false beliefs is the interpretation of values or how they are actually held. This means that what initially appeared to be a relatively objective standard—in seeming to be articulable and applicable independently of the potential suicidist's perceptions—is actually dependent on those perceptions. The upshot is that we seem not to have much of a basis for approbation or condemnation if all we have is an abstract statement of putatively operant values and the beliefs implied by that statement. For instance, recall the November 1978 "People's Temple" mass suicide in Jonestown, Guyana, which was prompted by the Reverend Jim Jones's rampant paranoia and which was surely one of the grossest misuses of religious doctrine and ministerial influence. Recall, too, how shockingly silent most religious leaders remained after the tragedy. That silence was likely prompted by fear of undermining their own doctrinal credibility and ministerial control, but it had a certain legitimacy. While disagreement with avowed Jonesian doctrines was perfectly in order, it was much more risky to condemn actions prompted by obviously authentic religious fervor. Jones and his pathetic followers certainly demonstrated the sincerity of their beliefs, however misconceived and dubiously related to published doctrines. There was less point than one might think, then, in being harshly critical of Jonesian doctrines as they were available to critics, since what mattered was how they were held and interpreted. And there was still less point in condemning the actions of obviously confused and deceived—and dead—individuals by criticizing their proclaimed doctrines. It would seem, therefore, that the requirement that a set of values be rational in not being based on false beliefs goes only some way toward enabling us to assess how those values actually function in a potential suicidist's reasoning. Even obviously flawed values may function in an acceptable deliberative way if their interpretation compensates for errors, and apparently rational values may function in an unacceptable deliberative way if their interpretation introduces errors. Is Narveson's requirement that values be well-grounded then superfluous? And must we accept that values are always subjective because as actually operant they are always determined by individual interpretation? Narveson's requirement is not superfluous because it does help us to attain a critical preliminary clarity. If we judge the values operant in a potential suicidist's deliberations to be not rational because of underlying false beliefs, we can reject the rationality of her suicide unless an interpretation of those values is provided which compensates for the false beliefs. As for the subjectivity of values, we are no worse off than we were before. In the end it is always the individual's interpretation of her values that matters in determining her actions. The important thing is that while we have to concede that her interpretation is decisive with respect to her decisions and actions, that is definitely not to say that we must *accept* her interpretation. We might well conclude that her values have not been rationally interpreted and that however exemplary her subsequent reasoning, her suicide is not rational if based on that interpretation.

Rational But Unreasonable?

We must now consider in more detail the most difficult aspect of the application of the values criterion. Our assessment of the rationality of the potential suicidist's interpretation of her values, and so of the role that interpretation plays in her deliberation, may be that the interpretation is unacceptable. But this may be so *even though* we can find nothing straightforwardly false in either the interpretation or the values interpreted, and seem obliged to accept them as rational. This possibility is evident in the case of the general, for we may concede that the priority the samurai code assigns personal honor over human life is in principle rational enough—in the thin sense—but still see the general's sacrifice of his life for his honor as not justified—as not rational in the thick sense. Our negative judgment may focus not on out-and-out falsity in the operant values or their interpretation, but on what we can describe as lack of proportion in their application.

Perhaps the best way to capture what I am suggesting here is to say that the unacceptability of the general's interpretation and application of his values is a matter of our perceiving undue exaggeration and depreciation of the importance of his values and interests respectively. More specifically, while we may accept and even appreciate the values operant in the general's suicidal deliberation, and acknowledge their rationality, we may think that he is being unreasonable, though not strictly irrational, in judging that his failures in a relatively minor role in the war effort require the sacrifice of his life—that is, require the terminal subjugation of his interests to his values. The point is the one anticipated a little earlier, namely, that suicide's having to be reasonable—or rational in *both* the thin and thick senses—means that it must not only be consistent with the values and interests of the agent, as required by the values and interests criteria, but must be so *in a balanced* way. Those persistent reservations about the general's suicide have to do with feeling that even if the consistency of his suicide with his values and interests is thought to be established, his interests are not being given their due weight.

What may make it look as if the interests criterion is satisfied, when the values criterion is satisfied, is that cultural values color the perception of interests. Given the samurai code, it will seem that a life of dishonor cannot be in the general's interests, even though continued life obviously is in his interests. A life of dishonor will be thought as contrary to the general's interests as a brief, pain-racked life is to a terminal patient's interests, and so as equally justifying suicide. The trouble is values determine what are best called *perceived* interests. And values and perceived interests usually contrast with *real* interests—at least where the latter can be discerned or defined (I return to the question of real interests below). Recourse to the admittedly somewhat fuzzy notion of reasonableness or thick rationality, then, can plausibly enough be characterized as resistance to letting values overshadow interests.

In using the notion of reasonableness we are in effect saying that a life of dishonor may be better for the general than an honorable but precipitated death, and that he would think so himself except for the powerful influence of his values on his perceptions and deliberations. The implicit claim is that samurai-code values are being allowed to unreasonably, though not actually irrationally, override the general's legitimate interest in continuing to live. Notice that the lack of balance could go in the other direction. That is, if an initial judgment were that a terminal patient would best serve her interests by committing suicide, some might feel that overly detached perception of her interests seriously discounts any antisuicidal values she may have.

What underlies resistance to letting the general's values prevail over his interest in continued existence is a strong tendency to rate continued life as the most special interest, the interest least readily overridden by value considerations. The question immediately arises, then, whether we are genuinely trying to maintain a proper balance in the consideration of the general's values and interests, or are only introducing a *different* set of values, one which assigns a higher place to continued life. This possibility is particularly evident in our case in point, in that we may not be culturally prepared to accept that any given case of samurai-code suicide is reasonable, even though we may concede the code's rationality in the abstract. This is just the possibility mentioned earlier, namely, that the rationality of suicide may be conceded at the abstract level but never accepted in particular cases. What likely happens in the general's case is that a Westerner finds the general was, after all, neither a traitor nor a saboteur. He made some mistakes; to die for those mistakes seems grossly disproportionate. This is the nub of the perceived unreasonableness: the general committing *sepuku* for the sake of a warrior's honor seems tragic excess, if not arrogant self-importance or mere foolishness. But to take this position may be only to reject the general's suicide, not because it is inconsistent with his interests, but because we are requiring consistency with *our* values. We must deal with the possibility that in the assessment of the consistency of suicide with values and interests, an appeal to reasonableness is introduction of different values. The way to do so is to produce a new criterion for balance or reasonableness to complement the nonimpairment, accessibility, values, and interests criteria. It may be possible to say how values and interests must be balanced in suicidal deliberation, without injecting different values into the equation, by devising a criterial test for reasonableness or thick rationality. However, while the new criterion for reasonableness may not introduce new values, it must presuppose a frame of reference broader than that of the general's own cultural and individual values, else it would be redundant because automatically satisfied by the consistency of suicide with his values. The easy way to justify this apparently problematic new frame of reference would be by plucking objective interests from a Platonic heaven or a Thomist human nature. But the broadening of the frame of reference is in fact no more problematic than that effected by implementation of *any* of the other criteria considered. While not necessarily making ahistorical claims, Battin, Choron, and Narveson must assume, in proposing their criteria, that standards of rationality are transcultural—though not necessarily *a*cultural. With respect to the proposed balance criterion, the basis of the transcultural claim about a fundamental interest in survival is that human beings, of whatever culture, are mortal entities, and so long as they are extant, they have a basic—though admittedly not absolute—interest in *remaining* extant. But human beings are also value-seeking entities, so their interest in remaining extant is not in mere survival as organisms—else remaining alive through elaborate technological support or while in nonending agony would raise no questions for us. This is the idea captured by the view that life's value is as the precondition of all *other* value (Hook, 1988). And this view is intuitively clear: for self-aware entities like ourselves, an interest in sheer existence is antecedent to, but inextricably wrapped up with, any value arising in experience. Our interest in remaining extant is not detachable from our ability to attain and appreciate value. And since death irrevocably finishes existence, willing termination of life—that is, abandonment of the interest in continued existence—is relinquishment of all possible value.

Culturally determined values will largely determine what is or is not judged worthier than survival, but the point here is that they cannot simply preempt or eradicate the interest in survival. This means that *value-driven* suicide can be rational and reasonable only if it either promises value outweighing all the agent's interest in survival and all possible future attainment of value, or is itself a valued way of terminally acknowledging that sufficient future value is no longer attainable. And what emerges in consideration of the general's *sepuku* is that attainment of future value is possible for him, and that his suicide does not achieve massive value as would, say, the sacrifice of his life in exchange for those of his troops. Therefore, what is at issue in assessment of the general's *sepuku* is the degree to which the general's interest in continued life should be subordinated to the demands of his samurai code. The introduction of a new criterion, then, must be a way of insuring that values and interests are properly balanced, that operant values are not being allowed to unduly overshadow interests—*or vice versa* (just as we do not want values to always force sacrifice of life, we do not want to preclude warranted sacrifice). While there is a danger here of too facilely contrasting real interests with perceived interests and values, we do need a way of gauging if something is going seriously wrong in suicidal deliberation when someone like the general seems too ready to sacrifice his interests—in terms of his very life—for his values. In a similar way, it is necessary to tell if something is going wrong when an individual too readily subordinates her values to her interests, for instance by preferring to commit some grossly immoral act rather than take her own life. Nonetheless, we do not want the requirement that values and interests be properly balanced to amount to a disingenuous introduction of philosophically unsupportable "objective" interests. The requirement must be no more than that willing abandonment of irretrievable life for the sake of specific values be supported with adequate evidence that those values outweigh the loss of all possible future value, or that future value is no longer attainable, or that it can be convincingly argued that still-attainable value is insufficient to constitute an interest in continued life.

The Reasonableness Criterion

The general's samurai code is the reason for his suicide, so his suicide is a sacrifice of interests for values. Nonetheless, even though we may acknowledge the possibility of rationally sacrificing life for values held, we may conclude that while the demands of the samurai code are rational in the abstract and *sepuku* appears to be a rational course of action for the general, still, as a sacrifice of his life and so of his most fundamental interest, his suicide is not reasonable. We judge that his interest in still-attainable value overrides the demands of his samurai code. But it is still not very clear what the basis and force of "not reasonable" are. It still *looks* as if we are discounting the general's values for cultural reasons, which would be to impose our own values. Things look a little clearer, though, when we say that what the judgment that his suicide is unreasonable really comes to is that we feel that the rationality gained for the general's suicide by satisfaction of the nonimpairment, accessibility, and values criteria is rendered incomplete or inadequate by suicide's violation of his most fundamental interest. The point would be that (assumed) positive assessment of the consistency of the general's suicide with his interests is faulty because too narrowly based or because it underestimates the importance of his interests and results in an imbalance in the weighting of his values relative to his interests. Our concern with reasonableness is not a concern with a separate and mysterious dimension of assessment. Reasonableness applies here not to the assessment of the separate consistency of suicide with interests, as opposed to its consistency with values, but to the *weighting* of interests. According to Battin's twofold understanding of the rationality issue, we would here be saying that while according to the samurai code *sepuku* is rational and called for, it is not rational for the general to commit *sepuku* because his interest in continued survival is *not* consistent with suicide when that interest is adequately assessed. The obvious objection will be that it still looks as if we are only smuggling in new values. However, the objection assumes that values have priority: that a case must be made for the interest in continued existence overriding the dictates of the samurai code. But the whole point of what I said above about our common interest in continued existence is that what is required is demonstration that the general's interest in living is overridden by the demands of his code in the given circumstances. That is, the onus is not on us to say why the general should be exempt from the samurai code's requirements; the onus is on him and his peers to show that errors of judgment as a leader merit sacrifice of his life.

We must not forget that the general's is only a case in point. I am not concerned to hammer out conditions for rational *sepuku*. The aim here is to see what emerges as most worrying in a case where it seems the criteria for rational suicide are met. In our discussion thus far I have stipulated that the nonimpairment and accessibility criteria are satisfied in the general's case, and clearly the values criterion is satisfied since the samurai code not only "recommends" but requires suicide. Nonetheless the general's suicide seems wrong; it seems not to be reasonable. And the likeliest ground for reservations is that it is not so easy to see how the general's suicide is or can be made consistent with his interests. It is important to pursue this reservation because the value of the general's *sepuku* as our case in point is that his is suicide prompted by values, not by terminal illness or similar desperate circumstances. It is therefore closest to the sort of suicide the reflective aging person discussed in Chapter 2 may deliberate about and commit. Our reservations in the one case are likely to be very similar to those in the other. We feel, in the general's case, that his priorities are skewed, so we are unwilling to accept his suicide as reasonable—though we may have to concede that as a type it is in some strict sense rational. This is very close to holding his values as themselves not rational because based on false beliefs. But it is only close, for when we try to articulate what we think false in his views, we find that what we articulate are precisely his values. For instance, we might say that the general falsely believes that personal honor requires his death as compensation for his failures. However, we cannot just claim that to be a false belief, because that is precisely the value centrally at issue. What we must mean, then, is that he is wrong to hold the code he holds, that he falsely believes it to be a code worthy of adherence and endorsement. But this is not to identify a false belief in or underlying the code. It is to reject the general's values on the basis of an alternative set. What we have to say goes something like this: we feel there is a serious imbalance in the general's thinking, in his assessment of his values and interests. This is not to say that we necessarily reject the operant values because based on discernible false beliefs. It is to say something rather more complicated, namely, that while we can understand how the general's suicide is consistent with his values, and so satisfies the values criterion, and we grant that the nonimpairment and accessibility criteria are also satisfied, difficulties emerge when we see that the general's suicide is consistent with his interests only if we downgrade those interests, relative to his values. That is, we do not accept the worth of his life (in the circumstances) as determined by his values.

What we need to do is prevent the interests criterion from collapsing into the values one. This happens if the interests criterion comes to be wholly internal to a given cultural or individual perspective, because that perspective will be shaped by precisely the values at odds with interests, and so will subordinate interests to values. The appeal to reasonableness or thick rationality is, first of all, an appeal for use of the broadest possible base for the construal and assessment of at least the most basic human interest, which is survival. Secondly, the appeal is for a balanced assessment of interests relative to values, particularly when values conflict with survival as an interest. We do not want the rationality and acceptability of suicide to simply follow from a potential suicidist's values and preferences. As in cases of assessing priorities in the distribution of goods, we want to make room for real interests, where "real" means only that interests are not simply identical with individual preferences or cultural values. Satisfaction of some interests, for instance, may be crucial to well-being even if unrecognized as such by some individuals and cultures. In a discussion of distributive justice, T. M. Scanlon reminds us that in comparing competing interests to make "a moral judgment as to which should . . . prevail," we do not limit consideration to "how strongly the people in question *feel* about these interests . . . " (Scanlon, 1975: 660).

Scanlon's concern is with competing interests, and is structured so that values are read as perceived interests opposed to independently justifiable interests, but his point is crucial to our discussion. If we are to distinguish at all between values and interests in discussing the rationality of suicide, interests have to be conceived as opposable in a significant way to what is prized or preferred. Interests must be construed, if not as "objective," then at least as having some basis beyond the individual's or her culture's values. Some interests must be construed as grounded in human traits, which—though not conceived in some essentialist sense—have been shown by our long history to generate requirements for the well-being of creatures like us. I have no doubt that our history supports various strong claims about what is or is not in the "real" interests of human beings, but since the relevant interest here is the sheer survival of the individual, there seems to be little need for arguments showing that interest to be basic. What needs stressing is that if only because continued survival is the condition of having and attaining values, survival cannot be taken as *unproblematically* vulnerable to negative evaluation. Certain of the individual's values may override her interest in survival, but there is no doubt that we can significantly oppose that interest to her values in deliberation of suicide. Her interest in continued existence, *even if ignored or repudiated*, cannot be rendered irrelevant or trifling by her or anyone else's values. The alternative is precisely to collapse the interests criterion into the values one and allow that the rationality of suicide turns only on consistency with values and *perceived* interests. And the bar to doing so actually has nothing to do with interests as such. The point is that if values and perceived interests are allowed to dominate interests, then the nonimpairment and accessibility criteria are effectively abandoned or at least seriously jeopardized. That is because clearly values and perceived interests would shape and determine what counts as nonimpairment and accessibility. To disallow meaningful opposition between values and interests is simply to turn the rational assessment of suicide into a futile exercise catering to prevailing individual and cultural values. And there is another point to be made here about the contrast between values and perceived interests on the one hand, and interests on the other. I began Chapter 3 by noting a difference between the common view that life is the ultimate value and worth preserving for its own sake, and the more sophisticated view that life is the precondition of all other values and is to be preserved so long as other values are attainable.

The first view considers the real interest in continued life as inviolable and so effectively an interest in existence *regardless* of other value. This is the position opposed to that which would automatically subordinate interests to values, as the samurai code possibly does. The second view, that life is the precondition of value, considers the real interest in continued life as primarily an interest in still-attainable value—for which existence is a prerequisite. It therefore tolerates the overriding of interests by values in some circumstances, though clearly its criteria for proper circumstances are a great deal more stringent than, say, the samurai code's criteria. Admittedly, even the first view may tolerate suicide if the value-content of continued life falls well below the neutral into the realm of continuous agony, but clearly the two positions differ most importantly on whether value-neutral existence is life worthy of continuation. And here we must understand "value-neutral" to cover both a vapid life devoid of any strong feeling as well as one where good and bad are somehow equally balanced. But the point is that no one who holds the view that life or existence is *itself* of supreme value could accept the possibility of suicide for principle—such as the general's *sepuku*—being rational. It would not be too much to say that for them preservation of life is itself the most basic principle of thick rationality or reasonableness. *Sepuku* and preemptive suicide in advanced age must remain incomprehensible to someone unwilling to consider the value of continued life in terms of life being only a condition for the attainment of other value. My debate about the reasonableness of suicide, then, must be with those who understand the interest in continued life as an interest in still-attainable value. Debate about suicide with those who think life is intrinsically valuable can only be definitional, in effect, since it would be a matter of arguing whether "rational" can cover willing forfeiture of existence. Donnelly's redefining of suicide to exclude euthanatic and ethically forced self-killing (Donnelly, 1978: 93) is an example of a basic maneuver in this latter debate.

My aim is to use the general's case to clarify the situation of the reflective aging individual who contemplates suicide, and whose contemplation of suicide is prompted not by desperate need but by considerations importantly similar to those operant in the general's case. In neither case is there unbearable torment; in both cases there is cool reflection on how what is most dear—honor and the respect of peers and subordinates; unimpaired reason and reflectivity—have been jeopardized. And just to the extent that our general and the reflective aging individual are free of immediate anguish, reservations arise about their suicides. Nor will it do to substitute psychological anguish for physical pain by stressing the distress experienced at the loss of honor or intellectuality, for that would be to change the cases in point. I am concerned with the rationality of preemptive suicide, not of escape from unendurable agony. The reservations about the reasonableness or thick rationality of the general's suicide are very like those we might have about the reflective aging individual's suicide because in both cases an irrevocable act is contemplated for what may seem to many to be inadequate reasons. The general seems to be sacrificing far too much, and the reflective aging individual seems to be acting precipitously. So far the best articulation of our reservations in the case of the general is that he may be giving undue weight to his values and depreciating his interest in continued existence. This articulation serves as well in the case of the elderly suicidist, because she may be overrating the importance of intellectuality and the danger to it, and radically underestimating how much good time she may have left. To make some progress, I shall now introduce the promised criterion. This could be a fifth condition labeled the "balance" criterion, in which case it could be stated as follows: suicide is rational if it satisfies the nonimpairment, accessibility, values, and interests criteria and, moreover, is consistent with both the potential suicidist's values and interests in a well-balanced way. But this would leave me with the need to clarify the sense of "well-balanced," which is just what we are finding difficult. A better maneuver is to introduce the criterion not as a separate one, but as a qualification to the values criterion. The expanded values criterion would read: suicide must be

3. consistent with the agent's operant, well-grounded values, without that consistency being gained by undue depreciation of the agent's interest in continued existence.

Admittedly "undue depreciation" is as difficult to clarify as "well-balanced," but at least the qualification operates on only one criterion rather than two, and is more specific in that it requires proper weighting of a particular interest. It might appear that having introduced this qualification, I need to introduce another qualification to the interests criterion, to the effect that deemed *inconsistency* of suicide with the potential suicidist's putative real interests—specifically her interest in continued life—ought not to simply preclude the rationality of suicide in cases where suicide is recommended by sound values and perceived interests. We want to guard against the potential suicidist's interests being objectified to a point where they preclude her values and perceived interests having significant import in any life-and-death decision. However, this further qualification seems too indeterminate to serve as part of the articulated criteria, given the diversity of values and perceived interests. It is the sort of consideration that would best be worked out in the application of the criteria. Note, too, that the need to speak of the inconsistency of suicide with real interests signals a lack of symmetry with respect to the consideration of the balance between values and interests. Whereas the exaggeration of values over interests is a serious problem in suicide, exaggeration of interests at the expense of values would be a problem more appropriate to euthanasia. That is, the other side of the coin to an agent's giving undue priority to her values, as might happen in the samurai-code case, is *third*-parties giving undue priority to an individual's interests on the grounds that those interests are best served by death regardless of her values. This is how a terminal patient's strongly held religious views might be circumvented in euthanasia. In fact, religious views are highly relevant here, because the sort of depreciation of interests which the balance qualification to the values criterion is designed to prevent is perhaps best exemplified in religious contexts. In these cases the individual's doctrinal values are enhanced, and her personal interests respectively depreciated, through indoctrination. The balance qualification is intended to insure that enhancement of values—and consequent easy satisfaction of the values criterion—do not result in too-ready satisfaction of the interests criterion. The values and interests criteria must insure that a positive or negative suicidal decision is proportionate to various factors: avowed values, individual interpretation of those values, perceived interests or interests determined by operant values, and real interests—especially the interest in continued life. There is, however, no suggestion that the balance qualification must insure that these factors are all equally weighted. Their being so would probably result not in rational action but in paralysis. The point of the qualification is to govern their *differential* weighting.

It would seem from what has been said that the criterial approach to establishing the rationality of suicide is least satisfactory with respect to the matter of the weight respectively assigned to values and interests in assessment of suicide's consistency with both. Since operant values will almost certainly be what initially prompt suicide in the cases that concern us here, the focus must be on the weight assigned to the individual's interest in continued existence—though certainly interests having to do with the quality of that existence must also be properly weighted. Unless the suicide being considered is prompted by an irreversible terminal condition, the potential suicidist's interest in continued life, and so in still-attainable value, will be seriously at odds with values and preferences prescribing suicide. This means that the main issue in all this is just what most people would anticipate, namely, whether the individual's value-generated reasons for committing suicide sufficiently outweigh her interest in continued life. But the familiarity of the issue does not answer the question of the *basis* on which we assess the balance of values and interests. The problem is to find enough common ground, between the potential suicidist and ourselves. We have to make our evaluation of her interest in continued existence less imposition of our values than proper recourse to a shared interest having equal significance for us as assessors and the potential suicidist as agent.

In this chapter I have attempted to clarify reservations about judging suicide rational on the basis of the satisfaction of criteria. What surfaced is that a major difficulty with the criterial approach is that satisfaction of both the values criterion and the interests criterion is complexly interrelated, and that while we may realize we need to achieve a proper balance in weighing values and interests, we are not at all sure how to do so. One thing in our favor is that the interest in continued existence seems so basic to extant but mortal creatures, that we feel we can have recourse to it as a common factor in assessing suicidal deliberation across a diversity of values and cultures. However, to rely overmuch on that factor would be to preclude the rationality of preemptive suicide of the sort that concerns me. This is because to the extent that we emphasize the objectivity of the interest in continued existence, we weaken the possibility of rationally choosing to die in the absence of great physical or moral threat. We must now more closely consider the question of interests. The question of proper balance between values and interests—specifically between values which prescribe suicide and the fundamental interest an extant entity has in continuing to exist—is essentially a question of how an individual's real interests *either* can be best served by her death, or fail to constitute a significant obstacle to value-driven suicide.

5

THE SUICIDIST'S INTERESTS

> There are . . . occasions on which a man should leave
> life . . . for reasons . . . not as pressing as they might
> be—the reasons which restrain us being not so press-
> ing either.
>
> Seneca, *Letters from a Stoic*

I shall begin consideration of how suicide may be in a reflective aging individual's interests by sketching a practical example. The general's case needs complementing by a second case in point capturing the reflective aging individual's special situation. Like the general, the individual here concerned is prompted to consider suicide by her values. Unlike the general, our representative aging individual is a few years beyond her "three score and ten." Our reflective aging individual faces three harsh facts at odds with her values: first, she has begun to notice some decline in her intellectuality; second, she has begun to outlive her friends and family of her generation; third, she is increasingly conscious of impending deterioration in health. A crucial consideration is that the detected decline in intellectuality does not yet amount to impairment of reasoning or, for that matter, decrease of reflectivity. The decline has to do with loss of interest, with a slowing of her thinking, and with an ominous increase of sentimentality. She finds herself more and more drawn to passive entertainment and less willing to tackle the issues and questions that so challenged her earlier; she finds that it takes her longer and longer to reach sound conclusions; she finds that more often than she likes she is caught up in memories of the past; she finds herself tending to put too high a premium on people's contentment and well-being, inclining to downgrade issues of principle. Additionally, she finds that her life now includes continuing loss as friends and acquaintances die and as younger family members move away or have less to do with her (Tolchin, 1989). There will no doubt be additional pressures, such as economic problems and growing difficulties dealing with much younger people who grow increasingly distant. The reflective aging individual begins to consider whether she should forgo Hume's "few years of infirmity" for the sake of dying on her own terms, in her own time, and before losing her intellectuality. She envisages a future in which she will be plagued not only by the ills and further losses that threaten, but by self-doubts and especially by regret that she did not end her life before losing her autonomy. Finally, the reflective aging individual realizes that as friends and close family members decrease in number, her personal responsibilities decrease even more. She has opportunities to volunteer her help and time, but more and more she finds the effort too great and the rewards of doubtful value. (Henceforth, the phrase "reflective aging individual" will refer to the representative figure in this example, as reference to the general has been and will continue to be to my first example.) This example will strike many as did that of the general: as not compelling serious consideration of suicide. The example certainly brings out the sadness that is our lot at the end of life, but as Beeman might insist, there is still value to be attained and insufficient reason to forfeit life. In a word, preemptive suicide will not be seen as in the reflective aging individual's interests.

The requirement that for suicide to be rational it must be in the interests of the agent, at least not harming the agent more than continuing to live would do, is probably the most important and difficult to satisfy. At its simplest, the issue is how suicide or personal annihilation could be better for someone than continued existence. In this respect the interests criterion is closest to the coherency-of-preference issue, for it tests the intelligibility of the idea that ceasing to exist may be the best option for an extant entity. The interests question can be put in striking terms: Can my death be good for me? When the question is put this way, one sees the strength of the view that the only time the answer could possibly be in the affirmative is when one is faced with an alternative so horrendous that avoiding it is worth the balance of life and all the value it might bring. The trouble this poses for my claims about the rationality and advisability of suicide in advanced age is that if the only benefit suicide achieves is avoidance of what threatens the agent, and if what threatens the agent is only anticipated—the actual harm being still in the future—then preemptive suicide must always be irrational or at least arational in being a disproportionate response to a threatening but still amorphous situation. And to make things worse, the threatening situation is one which the agent is only *unwilling* to bear, rather than one she will be *unable* to bear. The onus is on me, therefore, to show how preemptive suicide may serve the potential suicidist's interests, as surcease suicide serves the interests of someone in an unendurable situation.

Unfortunately, the literature on suicide is less helpful than it might be with respect to the suicidist's interests when they are not all but negated by a terminal condition. And while those who are antagonistic to volitional suicide sharply distinguish between values and objective interests, those who are more favorably disposed toward it tend to run together values and interests. For instance, in order to say how an agent's interests might be served by suicide, a central interest is often equated with or identified as the agent's most basic "project." This effectively detaches the central interest from the agent's own existence, in that way enabling death to serve her interests by best serving the project (Battin, 1982: 312). These projects are most often oth- er-directed, as with political or humanitarian activities, but they may be more abstract ones such as protection of principle—as in the case of Socrates. And while it is recognized that the projects may be personal, such as enhancement of the life of a child or younger friend, these projects blur the difference between the individual's values and interests by objectifying something valued. The alternative to equating interests with projects, and so with values, is to judge suicide rational only when it serves the agent's interests by preventing immediate pain and suffering. A somewhat more problematic version of this alternative is to allow that if a person knows herself and her limitations well enough, and cannot bear much hardship, the psychological cost of physical deterioration or serious changes in fortunes and lifestyle may justify suicide. This is to give due weight to psychological suffering and constant, plaguing dissatisfaction, and that is all to the good. But as I have noted several times, the rationality of *preemptive* suicide cannot be established by escalating one or another sort of disquiet or unhappiness to the level of agony required to justify *surcease* suicide. If the concept of preemptive suicide is viable, it cannot be of suicide as escape from anything; it must be as deliberate renunciation of life prompted by unwillingness to undergo certain transformations that appear to be inevitable if one goes on living. And these transformations are not of themselves agonizing as physical pain or extreme psychological duress are. For the reflective aging individual, these transformations include diminishment of her intellectual capacity and reflectiveness, dignity, and independence, but her suicide is not prompted by actual suffering. If it were, if all suicides resulted from mental or physical *torment*, then not only would there be no conceptual room for preemptive suicide, but the question of the rationality of suicide would be otiose, because suicide would always be an *effect* of unendurable suffering. It is also worth mentioning, more or less in passing, that the rationality of preemptive suicide should not be sought in Lucretian arguments which try to deflect injury to interests by maintaining that death is not harmful because, being dead, an individual can be neither harmed nor benefited. This is actually the positive version of the lack-of-contrast argument, since it trades on the non-state nature of being dead. I have never understood the supposed force of this way of thinking. It is certainly the case that once dead the individual, because nonexistent, cannot be harmed. But that seems an irrelevancy since as we saw in considering the lack–of–contrast argument, contemplating suicide is a matter of contemplating *dying*, not *being* dead. The only force Lucretian reassurances have is that one ought not to fear being dead, which is beside the point, as it is dying that is feared. Nonetheless, there is a tendency to use Lucretius's supposed "insight" that for the still-living death is not an evil—and that for the dead nothing is an evil—to stress that dying is a transition of no real importance. I find this Lucretian notion at best an expression of something like morbid hubris, and at worst sophistry. I agree with Battin when she says that "death is a harm" and adds that we must understand harm not just as "injury or discomfort, but also [as] . . . deprivation of pleasures, satisfactions, and other goods" (Battin, 1982: 308; Feinberg, 1984: 79–83). A suicidist harms herself or acts contrary to her interests in taking her own life, not only in a transient way through her self-inflicted dying, but because she thereby deprives herself utterly and irrevocably of "pleasures, satisfactions, and other goods." This is the force of the description of life as not *a* value but the enabling condition of all other value. This is also the force underlying the sanctioning of suicide in terminal illness, because in such cases the nature of anticipated experience has turned wholly negative and life has ceased to be the condition of value. In terminal illness life becomes the enabling condition of *disvalue*, of suffering without adequate compensation. To kill oneself in terminal illness is only to "deprive" oneself of suffering. But in preemptive suicide life has not yet become the condition of disvalue; it still offers enough compensation. Preemptive suicide, then, seems inescapably self-inflicted harm.

What prompts preemptive suicide is a deep unease. This unease, though powerful and heartfelt, is not actual anguish like physical pain and intense mental misery. There is little question that the unease *as such* does not justify forfeiture of life or make it consistent with one's interests. What must be clear about rational preemptive suicide is that instead of a forced choice, it is essentially a *trade*: time left to one is given up because of unwillingness to become something less than what one is. And it may be a fair enough trade. But it is as a trade that preemptive suicide must be shown consistent with one's interests if it is to be shown rational. And so far the only trade that looks to be rational is that of pain-filled time for the release of death. However, what prevents the notion of preemptive suicide from being obviously misconceived is that, as Seneca believed, what is forfeited in preemptive suicide may not be as dear as usually thought. Most people are convinced that only crushing pain or overwhelming moral threat sanction the forfeiture of life. But the key point in Seneca's insightful remark quoted at the beginning of this chapter is that the time given up in advanced age is not as precious as it once was. This is central to understanding preemptive suicide: a time comes when life no longer has the overwhelming value it once did. Far too much discussion of suicide turns on the assumption that life has a *constant* value which does not diminish but may be overridden when suffering becomes unavoidable, potent, and constant. Admittedly, Seneca's point does not go down easily. Too many will continue to think that life precisely does have a value that remains undiminished until life itself is lost, and that therefore life does constitute our most basic real interest.

"In One's Interests . . . "

There are at least four important senses in which we speak of somethings being in one's interests (Bond, 1988: 279). The least significant of these—except to the extent that it is often confused with the other three—is the sense of what satisfies desires or preferences. That is, if one prefers or desires something, it is in one's interest to achieve that something, just to the extent that we have an interest in satisfying our desires. However, this sense assumes that we always want what is good for us, or that we want it so badly that it takes priority over what is good for us, or even that no distinction can be drawn between what we want and what is good for us. This is the child's sense of "in one's interests," for children notoriously have difficulty accepting that what they want may not be to their benefit. We can call this the "satisfaction of desire" or simply the "desire" sense of "in one's interests." A second sense of somethings being in one's interests is that in which something is acknowledged as desirable, but is not in fact desired. This sense is more sophisticated than the "desire" sense, in that it acknowledges the possible discrepancy between desire and benefit. For instance, whereas the "desire" sense is best illustrated by the child who identifies her desires and interests, this second sense is well illustrated by the smoker in whose interests it is to stop smoking, but who may not want to stop. This second sense can be dubbed the "potential benefit" sense of being in one's interests. A third sense is that in which something is in one's interests in a given context or from some perspective. This sense is often central to disputes about interests, and is very close to being about values, since the perspective determining the nature of the interest is itself value-determined. In the general's case, for instance, suicide is in his interests in the sense that from the perspective of the samurai code, it is better for him to die an honorable death than to live in shame. This sense can be labeled the "perspective" sense of being in one's interests. The fourth sense of somethings being in one's interests, which we can call the "real benefit" sense, is the one that concerns us most directly. This is the sense in which something is in one's interests if it is in fact good for one, regardless of preferences or perspectives. This sense is admittedly somewhat problematic because of both "external" objections, which reject the sense altogether, and "internal" objections to its construal and implications. Those who press "external" objections reject the meaningfulness of the "real benefit" sense, arguing that the idea of something's being in someone's interests regardless of preference or context—in effect from any perspective, hence from no perspective—cannot be coherently made out. Those who press "internal" objections accept the meaningfulness of the sense in question, but resist objective or real interests, especially real ethical interests, arguing that such interests would make what is to one's benefit *obligatory*. The "internal" objections to real interests are mainly ethical concerns about the range of obligation, so do not immediately concern us. The "external" objection, that real interests are an essentially incoherent ahistorical illusion, is relevant here. As we have seen, the reasonableness reservation about preemptive suicide is the idea that such suicide unduly contravenes the potential suicidist's real interests, and so presupposes interests that are real in at least the sense made out earlier in which existent entities have a basic interest in continuing to exist. In the cases of the general and the reflective aging individual, we are disinclined to accept the rationality of their suicides mainly because we feel that their situations are not unendurable and so do not override their real interests, since those situations are only perceived by the potential suicidists as cause for suicide because of the determining role played by their respective values: personal honor in the case of the general and intellectual identity in the case of the reflective aging individual. Given the foregoing senses of "in one's interests," we can say that suicide apparently is not in their interests in the "real benefit" sense, only in the "perspective" and "desire" senses. But all of this assumes the viability of real interests. Now that we are clearer on the contrasts at issue, I must look again at how something is in one's interests in the "real benefit" sense.

Real Interests

Unless we are willing to postulate a Platonic heaven to house objective Good and objective human interests, reservations about the violation of real interests in preemptive suicide still seem to amount to the tacit introduction of other values. The alternatives allowed us seem to be only the two: unviable objective interests, or reliance on our own interest-determining values—as opposed to acceptance of the general's or the reflective aging individual's. We must consider a little more carefully remarks made in previous chapters about human beings having a real interest in continued life. The first thing to admit is that the sense of "real" at work here looks very suspicious in our present intellectual climate, given current impatience with anything that appears to entail ahistoricist claims. But fortunately, the incursion of contemporary historicist/ahistoricist and relativist/objectivist issues into our discussion is a less formidable problem than it seems. As has been said, there is no need to argue for a timeless "human nature" which generates equally timeless and inviolable interests, much less Platonic ideals. What I need to do is clarify what was indicated in the last chapter, namely, that the appeal to "real" interests is an appeal to the broadest possible basis for assessing conflicts of values and interests. Recourse to real interests is only attribution to human beings, and to all living beings, of an interest in continuing to live. The ground of the attribution is not something ahistorical but the understanding that human beings are mortal, and given that we now have little faith in notions of an afterlife, and that we have excluded such beliefs from suicidal consideration, it suffices that a human being is living for that human being to have a *prima facie* interest in continuing to live. Differently put, personal existence is a given, and when actual seems not to require justification for its continuance. It would if, for instance, its continuance was at the cost of the lives of others. But if no such condition obtains, and there is no other compelling condition like unbearable pain, it seems justification is required for the forfeiture of life and not for its maintenance. This point is most evident in the clearest cases of surcease suicide, where the *prima facie* interest in continued life is acknowledged by most to be overridden. Preemptive suicide poses the problems it does precisely because the *prima facie* interest in remaining extant is *not* clearly overridden by some punishing condition, so it is at least not obvious what suicide's justification may be. For my purposes, the notion of a real interest in continued existence is only that of a given against which we must show adequate cause for self-inflicted death. The notion of a real interest in continued existence is not that of an elemental feature of a sacrosanct human nature; it is simply the starting point for consideration of whether preemptive suicide is rational and/or advisable. To insist that either objective interests or particular values are being smuggled in by recourse to real interests is effectively to deny that the starting point for discussion of suicide should be acceptance of life and consequent requirement that good reason should be provided for its forfeiture. To pursue the objection is actually to claim that acceptance of life and the demand for good reason to disrupt that life are themselves problematic evaluative assumptions. But I do not see the force of this, because the alternative would be *not* to accept extant life as needing justification for its forfeiture. And that would be to allow self-inflicted death at will—or at most to restrict it to when consistent with sound values. It is noteworthy, though, that this alternative does not constitute a position contrary to mine, for it is to effectively deny the applicability or even the intelligibility of judgments about the rationality of suicide. This contention is an outright relativization of the propriety of suicide to individual values. The "real benefit" sense of "in one's interests" is only a requirement that we be able to say how an individual is better advised to die than to continue living, because *being* alive, she requires no special reason to *stay* alive.

Interests and Perceptions

The matter of real interests can be further clarified by considering the sorts of factors that properly worry us about someone taking her own life, especially in circumstances that are less than intolerable. Battin offers a statement of what is important in an analogous situation. Speaking of the restrictions on a depressed person's assessment of her options, Battin reminds us that her "judgment about probabilities may be seriously affected," that she may overemphasize the likelihood of negative events, "subconsciously suppressing data which lead to a more optimistic prediction" (Battin, 1982: 304). And it is not only the depressed person's perception of her future which is distorted; it is not only that "good things in the future tend to seem less significant than bad things occurring now." Her perception of the past is also affected because "depression tends to warp our recollections about our preferences" (Battin, 1982: 304). This means that long-held values and priorities may equally be skewed by depression and not allowed to play a proper role in the agent's deliberation. My concern is not with the depressed suicidist, but the reflective aging individual is prey to similar difficulties. She may fixate on certain features of her situation, as the general does with respect to personal honor, and thereby not give due weight to a still significant interest in continued life. The danger is that the reflective aging individual's perception and assessment of her probable future may be as much distorted by her values as the depressed person's view of her situation is by depression. We need recourse to real interests to enable us to argue with the reflective aging individual—or the general—without what we say being only an expression of our own values. Some, in considering the consistency of suicide with interests and in trying to more effectively argue against the forfeiture of life, try to understand life itself as a particular value (Battin, 1982: 309). This is the position that life itself is the supreme value, and as suggested, so reifies the interest in continued life that it precludes preemptive suicide—thus effectively ending discussion. If we are concerned to insure that a potential suicidist fully appreciates the real interest she has in what she may decide to forfeit, it is better to take the alternative position, which construes life as the condition of value (Hook, 1988: 22). By doing so, the interest in continued existence can be characterized not as an interest in a particular good or benefit, but an interest in continuing to be in a position to attain value, an interest in continuing to be able to have benefits accrue to one. Assuming that we can take the tautological as unproblematic, namely, that value is desirable, it clearly follows that it is desirable to be in a condition to attain value. This is precisely the sense in which an extant entity has a *real* interest in continuing in the state in which she may attain value. The general's case again illustrates the point. The trouble with allowing the general's values to justify his suicide is that, in the "real benefit" sense just clarified, his death seems to us not warranted by his values and perceived obligations. We think the sacrifice of his interest in remaining in a state in which he can realize value is too high a price to pay for his errors. We think the general is too devoutly concerned with his samurai code, that his values obscure his real interests by overemphasizing his interests in the "perspective" sense—and even in the "desire" sense, if he is sufficiently dedicated to actually *want* to die as his code ordains.

The way real interests outweigh perceived interests is clearest with respect to the "desire" sense. We are not prepared to accept suicide as rational if it is only consistent with the suicidist's interests in the "desire" sense. For one thing, someone might want to die while only temporarily despondent or carried away by some ideal. We cannot take momentary despair or short-lived idealistic exuberance as an adequate reason for suicide. Many of the errors the nonimpairment criterion tests for cluster around the "desire" sense, particularly in pathological cases. It is too easy for someone to misguidedly believe that suicide is in her interests because it is a quick way to a religious heaven or offers the satisfaction of being sorely missed, or because of a romantic muddle such as being "half in love with easeful Death" (Keats, 1955). We are prepared to grant that the general's suicide is consistent with his interests in the "perspective" sense because that sense allows satisfaction of Choron's accessibility requirement. That is, we can understand how suicide is in his perceived interests even though we find that consistency with interests insufficient because suicide does not afford the general real benefit. We are also prepared to consider that the general's perceived interests may be very powerful. But consistency of the general's or anyone else's suicide with interests in the "desire" sense is not a serious factor. This sense fails Choron's criterion because we do not understand how and why someone might want to die for reasons that could be shown inadequate by simply clarifying the agent's interests. In the case of the reflective aging individual things are not very different. The "desire" sense is equally insufficient, though we are prepared to concede that suicide may be in her interests in the "perspective" sense. But the contrast of the "desire" and "perspective" senses in which suicide might be in her interests, with the "real benefit" sense, is not as clear as in the case of the general.

Special Reasons

Given the nature of old age, there may be a certain falseness to claims that life is being forfeited too soon in preemptive suicide. This is where Beeman's objection looks as if it promises the elderly rewards which in reality are extremely dubious, not just with respect to their character and value, but their very possibility. The contrast with the general's case is instructive with respect to Seneca's insight about "the reasons which restrain us being not so pressing." In the case of the general's suicide there is a marked inclination, in balancing how things look to him with how they look to us, to heavily discount his values and preferences—and a reciprocal inclination to stress his real interests. If his future looks hopeless to him, it is largely because of his own views. We understand that proximity to a situation may tend to make things look too bleak to someone, and from a third-person perspective there seems always to be the conviction that a little forbearance will bring reappraisal, and so a change of heart. We expect that forbearance will lead to a more realistic appraisal of the situation and that the general will see how disproportionate it would be to sacrifice his life for his samurai code. He could then decide that the best course of action is to dedicate himself to rebuilding his ruined country.

I think the core of this antisuicidal inclination is that if the reasons for suicide are a matter of *perception*, of how the potential suicidist perceives her situation, they largely will not be accepted as sufficient reason to forfeit life. That is, suicide will generally not be thought adequately in one's interests if the interests served are "intentional" rather than "material." There are two points here: first, there is a marked tendency to discount "mere" perception or construal of a situation as stable enough to support a momentous decision; second, there is a rather different tendency to discount unease or unhappiness that has no compelling overt manifestations. The result is that if the condition that prompts suicide is a matter of how things look to a particular individual from a perspective not readily accessible to others—because of the primary role of personal perception and interpretation—that condition is thought too susceptible to change and is disallowed as a sufficient basis for a suicidal decision. The suffering of terminal cancer is palpable to others; whatever is experienced by the general or the reflective aging individual—or a Virginia Woolf—may be reflected in negative behavior, but it is not tangible enough to be taken as sufficiently onerous to justify suicide.

The strength of this attitude toward suicide was brought home to me by a television program in which the immediate family of a teenage suicidist were interviewed (*Currents*, 1988). Everything said in the half-hour discussion by the father, mother, older brother, and younger sister of the suicidist, had mainly to do with their profound bafflement about the suicidist's motives. The family's sorrow was either overwhelmed or perhaps in the process of being effectively displaced by astonishment at what had occurred. For instance, the mother awaited the autopsy report with the paradoxically hopeful expectation that it would show the presence of drugs in her daughter's bloodstream, and so explain the suicide. (The results were negative with respect to drugs.) The mother was even concerned that the suicide of a fourteen-year-old would prove so inexplicable as to reflect negatively on the family, because people would not find adequate reasons for the suicide and would speculate about conditions in the suicidist's home. All four family members expressed guilt for what were no doubt irrelevant factors, such as not being home at the time. It seemed that by accepting some measure of blame they were trying to explain the event, as if the basically trivial considerations they were raising proved the suicide had been spontaneous because of special opportunity, and so somehow inadvertent. No credit at all was given to the barely mentioned suicidist's unhappiness, and not one of the family members or the moderator speculated on the suicidist's perception of her own situation. It was simply unquestioned that a healthy fourteen-year-old *could not* have adequate reason to kill herself. The moderator closed by expressing hope for better understanding of the "causes, prevention, and tragic consequences" of suicide, as if she were speaking of a little-understood disease which people somehow contract and where volition and values play no relevant part.

In this case the suicidist's youth was the key factor preventing anything like a sympathetic attempt to understand motivation. In the case of the reflective aging individual, age will also prevent understanding, though in a very different way. It may be generally accepted that the old have better reason to die sooner rather than later, but in particular cases the tendency to discount or dismiss intentional factors proves to be the same. In the judicial commentary quoted in Chapter 3, the judge was not only discounting the seriousness of avowed preference for a natural if quicker death over a technologically sustained half-life. He was also reducing such avowals on the part of the elderly to merely "routine" or "expected" expressions on a par with lip-service paid to a superficially understood ideal. Even given some appreciation of the possibility that advanced age may be better cut short, individual perceptions are mistrusted on the grounds that no one can really want to die.

The perceived interest an individual may have in dying is so little regarded as a compelling consideration that our readiness to see overriding real interests outweighing perceived interests in suicidal deliberation must be highly suspect. At the same time, the negative attitude toward the significance of suicidal perceived interests is not without grounds, as we saw in considering real interests and the inadequacy of the "desire" sense of interests. Clearly we must proceed carefully. We can, though, sum things up as follows: as indicated, the "desire" sense of "in one's interests" is something of a nonstarter. We might allow that suicide must be consistent with it in addition to being consistent with the other three senses, but it is quite insufficient in itself. Suicide that was in one's interests only in the "desire" sense would not be rational because no reason for wanting to die which would be adequate could be accommodated by the "desire" sense alone. Given the magnitude of the contemplated act, any adequate reason for suicide would at least elevate the sense in which suicide would be in the individual's interests to the "perspective" sense. The "potential benefit" sense of "in one's interests" is also peripheral to our concern. There are no doubt cases where it would be in one's interests to commit suicide in spite of one's wishes, for instance, on being diagnosed as having a particularly virulent strain of Alzheimer's (assuming reliable diagnosis were possible). In a different sort of case, suicide would be in one's interests in the "potential benefit" sense if it could be known that crushingly tragic events were about to befall one. But the cases that interest us are those where the individual chooses to commit suicide, so the "potential benefit" sense is largely irrelevant. The "perspective" sense in which suicide may be consistent with interests is of primary concern for us both because it forces acknowledgement of the "real benefit" sense and because it is the main motivating element in preemptive suicide. In itself, though, this sense is not different enough from what is tested by the values criterion to merit more detailed treatment in its own right. To say that suicide is in someone's interests from a certain perspective is to say that given certain values, and certain conditions, suicide is in that person's interests to the extent that it is prescribed by her values and so is in her perceived interests—i.e., her interests as determined by her values. The "perspective" sense is also useful to bring out how perceived interests and values and the individual's personal assessment of her situation are usually thought separately and jointly inadequate to justify suicide or to show the consistency of suicide with real interests. But this is not the sense that must be vindicated. As we have seen, it is the "real benefit" sense that is decisive with respect to the rationality of suicide generally and preemptive suicide in particular. For preemptive suicide to be deemed consistent with the potential suicidist's interests, and thus judged rational (assuming satisfaction of the other criteria), we must be able to say how dying benefits the suicidist. And we must do so without changing the nature of preemptive suicide:

without turning it into surcease suicide by escalating the potential suicidist's misgivings about her future to a level of punishment equivalent to great physical or psychological torment.

So far, then, we seem to have an adequate sense in which living human beings have a real interest in continuing to live. And we are also clearer on how they may have a perceived or value-determined interest in dying. For suicide to be rational, it must be consistent with both interests, but to be consistent with a potential suicidist's real interests, it seems that continued life (as the condition of value) must cease to be a germane consideration because either no other value can be forthcoming, or not *enough* value can be attained. This articulation of the real-interests requirement captures the terminal-illness case quite well, and locates disputes about it precisely where they belong: in the context of determining whether an individual has deteriorated to a point where no other value can be attained. On a cursory analysis of preemptive suicide, it would be thought that in the general's case attainable value is antecedently precluded by his dishonor, that his code prevents the attainment of other value, hence his real interest in retaining the condition of other value is negated by his values. But we have seen that given the general's age and prospects, this view effectively collapses the interests criterion into the values one, giving rise to the reasonableness or thick-rationality reservation. In the reflective aging individual's case, what prompts consideration of suicide is fear that changes in herself will preclude or greatly lessen attainable value, so she too would be taken to have a strong perceived interest in dying which must negate or at least very much decrease her real interest in continued life. Both of these cases require that perceived interests or interests in the "perspective" sense be given special weight in the assessment of the consistency of suicide with real interests. Our question here is whether we have to draw substantially the same conclusion in both cases. That is, in the general's case we are most inclined to conclude that his real interests are not negated; does this hold true in the reflective aging individual's case too? At the very least we seem to be at a loss as to how to strike a proper balance between values and interests. Admittedly we may not find the general's views sufficiently plausible to try to establish that balance, but the reflective aging individual's case is a matter of age inexorably changing her by sufficiently diminishing her capacities so that she will not survive as the person she is. While we may be skeptical with respect to the general's values, it is harder to be skeptical about the consequences of living on for the reflective aging individual. For one thing, a real question arises about *who* has a real interest in continued life in her case. We may have to conclude that the reflective aging individual's real interest in continued life is dissipated to the extent that age changes her, and that what persists is only the *organism's* stake in continued existence, which cannot be understood as an interest in the relevant sense.

The Nature of the Choice

To better understand how preemptive suicide in advanced age could serve one's real interests, it is crucial to make clear the nature of the alternatives considered by the potential suicidist. The contemplation of suicide in less than desperate situations is not a matter of assessing whether continued existence, as the condition of all possible future value, is worth retaining in spite of extremely negative present or imminent factors. The alternatives are more subtle than that. In the case of surcease suicide the agent's existence is assailed by some condition or situation that is importantly extraneous to her, such as a terrible illness or a critical ethical choice forced on her by circumstance or malevolence. Her decision, then, must be whether to continue an existence now inescapably blighted by the intrusive element, or forfeit life in order to escape her predicament. But the reflective aging individual's existence is not so much assailed as it is *itself* changing in ways she cannot abide—though of course she may also be a victim of illness related to her age. The conditions that threaten her are not primarily external to her mode of existence; they are inherent to it as a temporal process. This is what many deny in arguing that old age as now conceived is a social construct. The point, though, is that what the reflective aging individual is considering is not continuing to exist and bearing a certain affliction or ceasing to exist and not bearing it. Instead she is considering whether to continue to exist as a *different* person or to cease to exist as herself. I ended Chapter 2 by saying that the reflective aging individual may decide that the person into which age is turning her is not one she thinks should live. That hard judgment is the heart of the decision to commit preemptive suicide in advanced age. It is not that the reflective aging individual cannot or will not bear some condition; it is that she will not bear *herself* as she is emerging in old age. But this means that future but still attainable value must play a very different role in her deliberation than in the suicidal deliberation of someone younger. The reflective aging individual realizes that the value which might still be attained will be effectively value for someone else. The changes she is undergoing will adulterate what she values, just as the general's dishonor is supposed to corrupt what he might still hope to attain. This is why both the general and the reflective aging individual assess the value continued life might bring more negatively than would a third party. Both assess what life might still offer as changed by their respective diminishment. Admittedly, the general's view of his future seems implausible to us, but it is hard not to be much more sympathetic to the reflective aging individual's understanding that though life will likely bring some compensating value even in very advanced age, that value may not be good enough, given that it will be value for her as a less intellectually capable and less reflective person than she is at present. The general and the reflective aging individual understand that suicide is less a choosing to die than it is a final affirmation of who and what they are at the moment of their decision. The decision the reflective aging individual makes in choosing to commit preemptive suicide is that she no longer *has* a real interest in continued existence, because she recognizes that her present existence, as the person she is and values being, is at an end, and that therefore existence as a condition of value is irrelevant to *her*.

A powerful counterargument against preemptive suicide in advanced age would be not something like the lack-of-contrast argument, but one to the effect that by continuing to live and struggling with what age brings, the reflective aging individual would become a *better* person—and not just in the moral assessment of others, but in her own experience. And this is in fact what many who oppose suicide in advanced age do argue. Donnelly, for instance, makes much of how bearing adversity can strengthen one's character and resolve, and how the adversity that is borne is actually alleviated by the greater tolerance and fortitude it itself fosters. Here adversity is treated as evil is treated when characterized as "first-order" evil in theological arguments against the inconsistency of God's claimed goodness and power with the undeniable presence of evil. First-order evil is supposedly justified by providing the occasion for "second-order" virtues such as moral courage. Allegedly, adversity in advanced age provides the occasion for fortitude—and so, to some extent, its own alleviation. But whereas harsh reality requires the development of second-order virtue, nothing requires individuals to bear personal diminishment in advanced age.

While there can be little question that dealing with adversity is a rewarding experience for some, it is so at least in part because of forward-looking benefit, namely, the strengthening of the individual. But bearing the sort of adversity faced by the reflective aging individual has no other point than learning to tolerate *more* adversity. The elderly individual is no longer in a position to benefit in the future from courage and forbearance in the present. All that coping with adversity comes to in her case is enduring that much more deterioration. In this respect the general is much better off. It is possible for him to choose to bear and try to overcome his dishonor by ignoring the demands of his samurai code and instead devoting all his energies to working for his defeated country. That way he may reach a point where he feels he has atoned for his failures by putting his jeopardized life to good use, thereby satisfying the demands of his values with respect to his personal honor without committing *sepuku*. But there is nothing the reflective aging individual can do that is comparable. The demands of her values cannot be met with some alternative course of action. If she continues to live her values will be violated by diminishment resulting from her own survival. This is the crucial point: a major component of the reflective aging individual's values is *being* the person she is, and valuing everything *else* as the person she is. It is her very survival that now threatens those values.

The deterioration age brings cannot be stopped or reversed through effort, as the general's dishonor may be expunged through service. There are exercises for memory, and recommended practices for maintaining one's interest in world affairs, as well as the now ubiquitous discussion groups that at least provide some measure of support, and one can always follow research news in hope of improved or new drugs, but these are inconsequential matters. They change nothing, at best offering solace through distraction and the illusion of effectiveness. Faced as she is with inevitable deteriorative change in herself, the reflective aging individual's choice is one between dying now, as herself, or enduring the slow diminishment of her *persona* and dying later as someone else. And the conditions that generate this choice in effect negate *her* real interest in continued existence more surely than the general's dishonor is supposed to turn value he might attain to proverbial ashes in his mouth.

The Nature of What Is Left

Once we understand the nature of the choice facing the reflective aging individual, we have half of what we need to appreciate the reduced nature of her real interest in continued life. That is, we will understand that life is for her the condition of still-attainable value only in a Pickwickian sense, because the value that may accrue to her as an organism will not necessarily accrue to her as the person she is now. The other half of what we need has to do with the nature of remaining life. And we can get at that by recalling that the crucial difference between the general's case and that of the reflective aging individual is that while the general is in his late forties or early fifties, and so sacrifices a substantial future in committing suicide, the reflective aging individual's future as an intentional being is very limited, and her future as an organism is determinately negative. Whether for a person or an organism, the central fact of advanced age is the "hard fact of having come to the end" (Blythe, 1979: 5). As Blythe tells us, "when the old say . . . 'I simply can't go on,' they are stating their major frustration, not announcing a coming to terms with death" (Blythe, 1979: 5). While preemptive suicide in advanced age bears important similarities to other value-dictated suicides, such as the general's *sepuku*, it is very different precisely because of the limited nature of what the elderly person forfeits. If we pursued the general's case we would probably conclude that his suicide is in fact not rational, that his real interests do outweigh the demands of his samurai code. And most likely that would be because the reasonableness qualification is not met.

Age clearly matters a great deal here, in that the qualification cannot be met if what is forfeited is of a certain measure. For instance, could we imagine judging *sepuku* rational if contemplated or committed by a twelve-year-old? As in the teenage suicide mentioned earlier, we have to be prepared to believe that an adolescent's suicide may be justified, but we would certainly reject the idea that considerations of personal honor suffice to justify *sepuku* by a child or an adolescent. What someone in her first or second decade forfeits in suicide far outweighs whatever dishonor she might be capable of at that age. Even given gross despondency and shame, we would not accept the rationality of her suicide if considerations of personal honor were its grounds—though we might have to accept other grounds as adequate. And what is clear is that the dominant factor in our assessment of a child's or an adolescent's suicide is precisely her age.

Against this, assessment of the real interest an elderly individual has in continued life must be heavily influenced by the nature of advanced age. Though there certainly are people who live even into their nineties in relatively good health and with unimpaired mental faculties, and in spite of the fact that modern nutrition and medicine have made the quality of life of our seventh decade comparable to that of our parents' sixth decade, a realistic view is that most of us who live beyond our late sixties and early seventies will have relatively short, bleak futures. As Battin puts it, "we will lose control not just over our pocketbooks and our bladders but over all the major circumstances of our lives." And she adds the most telling point: "There will be no recovery from this condition" (Battin, 1987: 162). But even Battin's stark remarks miss the more central loss discussed in the last section. Her use of "we" suggests that it is *we*, the persons we are at fifty or sixty, who will endure the woes she lists. But by that time we will be who we were when younger only intermittently, if at all. In spite of her toughmindedness, Battin here lends unwitting support to the basically religious myth of the essentially unchanged person trapped in an aging body.

Since I began researching aging I have been repeatedly depressed by items in this vein usually offered as inspirational. What I have in mind is exemplified by the sort of letter or poem written by very elderly nursing home patients to the effect that they are themselves not the incontinent and powerless husks their nurses tend. These efforts to salvage self-respect, no doubt written in moments of clarity and frustration, are less reassuring than they are piteous. Though much loved by the media and much used by all those concerned to cheer and reassure, these articulations of brief recapturings of former abilities in no way change the reality of their authors' plights. The bleak future of advanced age must be recognized as not something that may befall one, and which can afflict one without deep change. Rather it is inherent to the process of a life's ending. It is not that what we will endure in advanced age is an affliction which may make us willing to forfeit life; life itself comes to be unappealing in gradually ceasing to be both the condition of attaining value and the continuation of the *same* individual.

As noted earlier, most people think of life as maintaining a constant value as the condition of other value and as the continued existence of a given person—though the latter point is so taken for granted that it is almost never articulated. But human life is not just an enabling condition; it is an ongoing process of organic growth, maintenance, and eventual slow disintegration. The confusion which construes the bleakness of advanced age as an unfortunate but intrinsically "accidental" property is a legacy of our culture's religious history. If one sees oneself as an embodied spirit, then continued existence is a unique and unqualified condition, and adversity in advanced age will look to be something which the spirit must endure because of the nature of its embodiment. We must understand that we are bodily entities, and that the adversity of advanced age is deterioration in *ourselves*, not only in our corporeal circumstances. But to return to the point, Battin's remarks at least do capture the bleakness of old age even if endured by a person largely undiminished in herself. Admittedly some, like Hume, retain most of their intellectuality and general disposition to the very end, probably through good fortune in the nature of their final illness and other difficulties. But something very important must be acknowledged before comfort is taken in that possibility or it is used to attempt to refute claims about the inherent nature of age-related decline: Those who age and die like Hume start out with rather more than most others. Their decline is relative to their native ability, disposition, and intellectuality. We must understand that deaths like Hume's—or that of the mythical grandparent who slips away peacefully, surrounded by friends and family and dispensing wise homilies—are so rare as to not constitute anything remotely like a practical possibility. To be prepared to risk years of diminishment and great discomfort on the off-chance of such an old age and death is to make a fool's wager. In fact, some believe that when we have changed present cultural attitudes toward suicide, and better understand the realities of the advanced ages more of us now attain, we will not need to justify suicide with extreme suffering or moral threat. Suicide will in fact become the *preferred* way to end one's life, because it enables us to die on our own terms and in our own time (Kastenbaum, 1976).

Nonetheless, deterioration in advanced age is relatively slow, some accommodation to it can be made, and there are specific values which are outstanding enough that they may retain their worth and serve as important goals for even those who have lost a good measure of their capacities—for instance, an anticipated event such as the birth of a great-grandchild, or some notable achievement such as human beings landing on Mars. It is all very well to talk in the abstract about ceasing to be the persons we are, and about being plagued by Battin's inventory of woes, but in practice as we age we adjust to what even a few months before we would have rejected as intolerable. People are immensely adaptable. This is precisely what the reflective aging individual fears, that she will make too many adjustments and lose her intellectual identity without realizing it. But the point is that the real interest in continued existence does not simply evaporate at the first indication that age has begun to diminish us. While the reflective aging individual may be on her guard against personal deterioration, she may still have important hope for her future and so a real interest in continued life. The pivotal consideration, then, is that if it is rational to maximize one's benefits, then, even if we accept the rationality of preemptive suicide and the importance of the reasons for it, it would not be rational to do anything *too soon* that would preclude the achievement of benefits, which is precisely what preemptive suicide may do. Choosing to die seems to require rather certain knowledge of both our present condition and of what our futures will be like, to justify the judgment that we are forfeiting only what is largely not worth having for the sake of death on our own terms. Can what we know about the *likely* character of our own old age suffice to make the forfeiture rational? At this point one might be tempted to take the Lucretian line noted earlier and argue that suicide is not against one's interests because the suicidist will not experience the consequences of her act (Martin, 1980: 148-49; Battin, 1987: 163). However, as indicated earlier, death is undeniably a harm. We are left, then, with the question of how the reflective elderly suicidist assesses *when* she ceases to have a significant real interest in remaining alive. As noted in Chapter 1, it may be that there simply is never a moment when she can say: "I should die *now*."

Obviously the reflective aging individual must consider suicide when she is advanced enough in age that age-related deterioration can be assumed to have begun, even if it is not yet noticeable. But she should not be so advanced in age that her deliberation is no longer reliable or she has lost the requisite autonomy to enact a suicidal decision. A second, perhaps less obvious, point is that the natural bent people have toward optimism or pessimism clearly is an important consideration with respect to suicidal deliberation. As was indicated in Chapter 1, consultation with friends and professionals will prove crucial and possibly decisive in the consideration of preemptive suicide. It will be all-important for the potential suicidist to have the advice of others with respect to the timing of her deliberation, because her optimism or pessimism may seriously distort her own perception and appraisal of her situation. She will also need authoritative information on her mental and physical condition, as well as the best available evidence of how genetically-close relatives fared in old age. The suicidist is considering a trade of time left for the avoidance of what that time likely will bring, so the basis for her decision must be as solid as possible. The fact remains that part of that basis will be little more than an educated guess about her future. As Donnelly and others would point out, not everyone's old age is a living hell, and no one can know what is in store for them purely as functions of chronological, biological, and social age. Nonetheless, there is abundant evidence that beyond a certain point, survival becomes mere survival in the sense that the life of a very elderly person comes to be a series of worsening trials, diminishing autonomy, and decreasing understanding and awareness. And as noted in stressing the difference between the cases of the reflective aging individual and the general, things will not get better for the aging individual. What is forfeited in hastening death, therefore, is best conceived as a number of relatively stable periods of minimal difficulty which will afford opportunities to attain the value suicide precludes. The compensation a later natural death offers for the risk it entails is the chance of periods of time during which life may still be relished. But it must be understood that even barring personal diminishment, one's real interest in continued life begins to decrease precipitately in advanced age because of the likely negative character of the time left. The only question for the reflective aging individual is when that decrease reaches a point at which attainable benefits are outweighed by the risk of both serious difficulties and the onset of significant personal diminishment. The upshot is that the realization that one's real interest in continued life decreases with age, that, as Seneca puts it, our reasons for continuing to live become less pressing, itself does little to resolve the question of when that interest reaches a practical minimum. However, the realization does break the grip of the erroneous idea that the interest in continued life is an unchanging one, that the value of life is an absolute value which can only be *overridden*. The value of life fluctuates, as does any other value, with respect to circumstances. So we have made some progress. In this and the previous section we have gained better understanding of the sort of choice faced by the reflective aging individual, and how she must construe the interest in continued life, which seemed previously to rule out preemptive suicide and so deny her that choice.

A Recapitulation

Two different points about an elderly suicidist's interests are intertwined in what has so far been said, as they must be intertwined in the reflective aging individual's suicidal deliberation. First, there is an important sense in which the reflective aging individual's real interest in continued existence is not identical with her real interest in continued life as an organism. The point here is that we do not survive quite as long as our bodies. While I most certainly do not want to endorse some form of dualism, it seems clear that as intentional beings, as entities who are subjects of experience in determinate ways, we are products of delicate and complex neurophysiological structures and processes. For most of our lives our intentional existence is adequately supported by the underlying neurophysiology, though obviously all sorts of things go wrong, from imbalances causing schizophrenia to transient changes causing barely detectable shifts in mood. But as our bodies begin to deteriorate toward the end of their functional life spans, our intentional existence is no longer as reliably supported or as stable. The reflective aging individual realizes all of this, and understands that *she* will almost certainly cease to exist as the person she is some time before her body actually dies. The choice she faces, as we saw above, is not simply between dying by her own hand or naturally. She faces a choice between dying as *herself* or eventually dying as someone less than herself. Her interest in continued existence is therefore a complex one. Its major component is an interest in continued existence as an intentional being, and its minor component is an interest in the continued functional existence of her body. The import of all this to the assessment of the rationality of her suicide is that when we consider if her suicide is consistent with "her interests," we have to be clear what it is we are weighing. We could, for instance, think it likely a given elderly person's body will live for a fair number of relatively healthy years, and therefore that she has a significant and real interest in continued life. But for some neurophysiological reason, such as Alzheimer's disease, her projected life as an intentional entity might be measured in weeks. Her suicide then would properly be considered in terms of surcease suicide in a terminal condition, and we would be wrong to assign much importance to her expected physical duration as an organism. The consequence would be that her values and perceived interest in dying would be decisive, and acknowledgement that her suicide is not consistent with her *body's* projected life span would be a relatively minor consideration. What has to be appreciated is that where age itself threatens the intentional existence of the reflective aging individual, the fact that her body may have a substantial projected life span does not mean that the reflective aging individual therefore has an interest in continued life—i.e., one coincident with that projected life span. Just as in the former case we would discount that projection as not generating a significant real interest, in the latter case we should also discount that interest. And we should do so for two reasons: the existence of the intentional being in question is not coextensive with that of her body, and in any case the projected life span is not of the requisite quality to generate a significant interest in continued life. This second point is that in advanced age an individual's future is most likely a limited and bleak one, so the elderly person forfeits much less in choosing to die in her own way and at her own time, even if she could reasonably expect to live on for a number of years without serious diminishment of her intentional identity. This is, of course, Seneca's and Hume's point. Here again, then, when we consider an elderly potential suicidist's interests, we must be careful not to treat them as having an absolute value, or the same value as they have for a younger individual. Arguments such as Donnelly's against the rationality of suicide invariably ignore this aspect of the question. As noted earlier, the assumption is that life, hence the real interest in continued existence, has a determinate and absolute value regardless of the age of the potential suicidist.

We might now rephrase some of the foregoing as follows: in the case of the elderly potential suicidist, the requirement that there be proper assessment of her interests in judging whether her suicide is rational is basically a matter of establishing whether there exists a significant possibility of value attainment for her as the intentional being she is. It is only if there is such a possibility that there is a sufficient counterpoint to the reflective aging individual's value-prescribed suicide. That is, it is not the balance of her life as an organism that constitutes an interest for the reflective aging individual. What makes that balance a potential interest is that it may afford time in which she may continue to be the person she is, and may afford opportunities for attaining value in spite of the increasingly negative character of her life as an organism. This point is most easily seen in the readiness with which we judge suicide consistent with an individual's interests in a painful terminal condition. Due to there being no possibility of improvement, and the punishing circumstances of the condition, life in a terminal situation ceases to constitute an interest for its bearer *regardless* of its potential length. As human beings age, the interest in continued existence changes from an interest in existence itself, to an interest in existence as more and more qualified by both identity considerations and value requirements. The value of life is neither absolute nor totally a function of the quality of that life; instead it is a dynamically changing function of identity, quantity, and quality. The value of life begins as a quantitative asset, a matter of the greatest amount of time and possibility. At the beginning of life the very promise held out by the amount of time left reduces the importance of its immediate and short-term quality, because that quality is compensated for by the possibility of significant improvement. But with advancing age life becomes more and more a qualitative asset. The lessening of the possible time left intensifies the importance of quality. The real interest in continued life is in fact not an interest in what we can describe as sheer duration. As extant mortal creatures we have a real interest in remaining extant. But we are not only extant: we are self-aware, thinking, feeling beings, and continued existence means continued existence *as the same persons* and with at least minimal levels of satisfaction and gratification. Both of these requirements escalate in importance as the time left to us grows short, and sheer duration neither constitutes life for us nor generates a real interest in its continuation.

We seem, then, to end up where we might have anticipated, namely, judging that the consistency of suicide with interests depends on the nature of those interests. Nor should this surprise us or make us feel that we have labored too hard for too little return. As always in philosophy—*pace* Marx—we end up where

we started, but with better understanding. I can summarize
that understanding as follows: in considering the consistency
of preemptive suicide with the potential suicidist's interests, we
begin with a given, namely, the real interest an extant entity has
in remaining extant. But that given must be qualified by the likely
quantity and quality of continued existence, where the relation
between quantity and quality is an inverse one: as the quantity
goes down, the quality must go up. That given must also be
qualified by careful appraisal of whether significant deterioration
of the *person* is likely. The greater the negative change, the less
likely it is that the surviving individual is the same as has
previously lived, meaning that she has already largely lost her
real interest in continued existence.

What complicates the foregoing is that the final assessment of
the satisfactoriness of continued existence is, after all, made by
the individual affected. One aging individual might well decide
that she will accept quite a high degree of mental and/or physical
diminishment for the sake of continuing to live. Again, another
aging individual may not be willing to tolerate even slight
diminishment. The willingness or unwillingness in question may
be modified to some degree by education and frank discussion of
the realities of the situation, but we could not force a judgment
on anyone. Must we in the end acknowledge that values and
perceived interests are what count, and that real interests are no
more than a starting point for discussion and assessment? I do
not think this to be either a trivial or a disappointing conclusion
to reach. We *do* have a real interest in continued existence, and it is
crucial to acknowledge and respect that interest. In the case of the
general the point can be pressed very hard in arguing against his
value-prescribed suicide, and as we saw above, it can be pressed
even harder in the case of an adolescent choosing to die for what
are in her case immature reasons. But we have learned that the
point cannot be pressed nearly as hard in the case of an elderly
person. Her real interest in continued existence is only a starting
point for deliberation because there is also precisely as Seneca
says: a much less pressing reason to go on living.

6

A MATTER OF TIME

> Judging whether life is . . . worth living amounts to answer-
> ing the fundamental question of philosophy.
>
> Camus, *The Myth of Sisyphus*

My aim in the preceding chapter was to show that in advanced
age a person's real interest in continued existence is a qualified
one. Given the reduced nature of that interest, it is plausibly
arguable that the inconsistency of preemptive suicide with the
basic interest in continued life is not of itself a bar to rational
suicide in old age. As we saw, in advanced age the importance
of the agent's interest in continued life declines in proportion
to the shortening of her remaining life span. That time not
only threatens personal diminishment and grows too short to
compensate for the threat, it will also be increasingly marred by
the powerlessness, afflictions, and discomforts which characterize
old age. While not necessarily diminishing in themselves, these
latter age-related burdens do temper our interest in continued
existence. Of course the inconsistency of suicide with the interest
in continued life may be resolved by a punishing condition
which reduces that interest to an insignificant degree, but if
this occurs we would be dealing with surcease suicide, not
preemptive suicide. Preemptive suicide in fact *requires* that
there be some inconsistency between suicide and the agent's
interest in continued life, since it is precisely the forfeiture
of viable time for the sake of avoiding the dangers which

that time entails. This is why it is necessary to show that the potential preemptive suicidist's interest in continued life can be rationally renounced because of negative assessment of her prospects. In surcease suicide one needs to show only that the potential suicidist no longer has an interest in continued life because of a terminal condition, or that her interest is wholly overridden by some unendurable situation or inescapable moral danger. It is an essential aspect of preemptive suicide that the agent not have compelling reasons for suicide, and so have a genuine choice to make with respect to deliberately forfeiting the balance of her life.

Never a Benefit

To show that preemptive suicide in advanced age can be rational in spite of contravention of the suicidist's fundamental interest in continued life—because of the lessened importance of that interest—is not to show that suicide advances the individual's interests in any straightforward sense. Suicide of whatever sort cannot *benefit* an agent in the sense of being an act which improves her situation, since the immediate consequence of suicide is cessation of the agent's existence. This is the point which Donnelly's lack-of-contrast argument uses in a confused manner, namely, that there is no sense in which we can say that an individual who commits suicide is *then* better off. The most we can say is that the individual is "better off dead" in the sense that it was preferable for her to cease to exist than to continue to exist under the relevant specifiable circumstances. The only way suicide can be in one's interests is by enabling the suicidist to avoid something, whether it be personal diminishment, or suffering inadequately compensated for, or an ethical dilemma. This point seems clear enough, and nothing I have said should suggest I am arguing for the mad idea that suicide can actually improve things for the agent. As Battin reminds us, death is a harm, and since clearly contrary to interests, self-inflicted harm is justified only if the alternative is worse. What is centrally at issue with respect to preemptive suicide is whether negative value-judgments about threatened future conditions amount to a worse alternative to continued life, and so justify self-inflicted

death in the way unendurable or terminal circumstances justify
surcease suicide. The key difference between preemptive and
surcease suicide is that the former is decided on and committed
in the absence of the sorts of pressures that occasion the latter,
so preemptive suicide always contravenes the agent's interests
to whatever extent her life is and would continue to be relatively
free of those pressures.

Assuming that the gist of what was said in the previous
chapter is right and a minimal contravention of the interest
in continued life can be rational, we seem to require a way of
establishing *when* preemptive suicide contravenes that interest
to the least possible degree. Or, more realistically, we need a way
of establishing the temporal context for a sound judgment to that
effect. That is, given that some contravention of the agent's real
interest in continued life is rationally justified by threatened—as
opposed to actual—diminishment, that contravention will have
to be so timed that it is as minimal as it is within our power to
determine. Even though the reflective aging individual's interest
in continued life is of a reduced sort, it is still an interest. In
surcease suicide the matter of timing is largely resolved by the
very circumstances that prompt the commission of suicide. There
may be some question about a matter of hours, or perhaps of
a day or two, in order to do something like prepare a will or
get information on a promising new treatment, but these are
minor considerations. The whole point of surcease suicide is
to escape what has already befallen one, so there is no deep
issue about when surcease suicide should be considered and
committed. Against this, in preemptive suicide timing is an
essential consideration precisely because preemptive suicide
must be considered and committed prior to imminent or actual
terminal pressures on the agent. To act rationally in committing
preemptive suicide, one must leave as little time as possible
between taking one's life and the likely onset of whatever
diminishing condition is feared and which would by its nature
either preclude rational suicide or allow only surcease suicide.
Regardless of what other criteria may be satisfied, preemptive
suicide could not be rational if committed too soon, for that would
be to sacrifice more of life than necessary and to excessively
contravene one's interests by robbing oneself of value. It is

rational to maximize benefits to oneself, so as much as possible
must be gotten out of life before it is surrendered voluntarily. We
might paraphrase Camus and say that the fundamental question
in the present context is determining *when* life is no longer
worth living. We need, then, a temporal criterion or temporal
qualification to one of our criteria for rational suicide.

Other Aspects of Timing

   The matter of timing raises anew our fundamental coherency question because the coherency of preferring to die has an
essential temporal dimension. To prefer to die, with "vivid
awareness" of what dying entails, must be to actually have
a preference for death at some particular time. That is, I do
not mean the agent must have a preference to die at a given
time, say on her seventy-fifth birthday, but that she must at
some given time form the preference to die either then or in
the immediate future. What is required is not just a death date
but actualization of the preference for death. Full understanding
of what it is to bring about one's own death requires more than a
general readiness to commit suicide under certain circumstances
at some unspecified future time or at a specified but distant
time. It requires that someone having the general preference
and intention to die, rather than risk personal diminishment, at
some point acknowledges that the question of whether to enact
her suicidal intention has become *current*. The agent may decide
not to take her life, but there can be no full understanding of
the nature and consequences of suicide if the suicidal preference
is not actualized at least to the extent that suicide ceases to
be a future option and becomes an immediate one. Without a
specific and fairly close temporal focus, the preference to die
remains too abstract to have Harman's "vivid awareness" of
consequences. There is a critical difference between having an
abstract preference for death over diminishment or dependency,
and actually having that preference when there is convincing
evidence that one is becoming diminished or dependent. This
point is the real force behind the sort of thinking exhibited in
the judge's dismissal of expressed desires to forgo life-support
which I referred to in Chapter 3. Judge Wachtler was right to

the extent that we cannot simply take avowals made prior to actual need of life-support as being equivalent to rejection of such support when dependent on it.

The requirement that preemptive suicide be deliberated at a particular time raises a related temporal consideration about when in an individual's life that deliberation can be undertaken with full understanding of the consequences of suicide. It is probably safe to say that one must have lived to a mature age before such understanding is possible. A proper understanding of death presupposes a fully adult understanding of life. What is tragic about most adolescent suicides is that the suicidists have an incomplete understanding of what they are giving up. They have simply not lived long enough. For instance, they will not understand that time will eventually offer a new perspective on whatever prompts their suicidal thoughts, nor do they know enough about the compensations life undeniably provides for much of what we must endure. If there is to be a coherent preference for personal annihilation, one must have lived long enough to understand the nature of what is forfeited. And the need of a capacity for mature judgment raises another consideration, though one having less to do with time itself than with how time is used. The consideration is nonetheless relevant here because of how the use of time colors our perception of present and future. It is likely that an individual's depth of understanding of the annihilatory consequences of suicide exists in some sort of inverse ratio to the positive character of the individual's experienced time. In fact, once said, this seems something of a truism. We certainly know that despondency in illness or any other condition that isolates and idles us makes death easier to consider, if not to face. If one's time is filled with satisfying activities and enriched with rewarding relationships, it is no doubt more difficult to think deeply on death. Death and deterioration seem to come as surprises to the happy and busy, and it may be that a strongly cheerful disposition combined with a very active life does make unlikely, if it does not preclude, the possibility of rational preemptive suicide. Certainly optimism and busyness would inhibit effective suicidal deliberation; they may obstruct such deliberation as much as depression inappropriately encourages it. But it is hardly only the idle and lonely who may decide on preemptive suicide. Nor could the reflective aging individual's choice to forfeit life be born only of despondency, since that would also jeopardize the rationality of her decision. Seneca and Hume again provide excellent examples of what is called for: in contrast to Nietzsche's forceful (but moot) desire for a "free death," Hume and Seneca manifested a *readiness* to die after long, productive lives. Theirs was a preparedness for death that arose not only from their respective ages and conditions, but from attainment of a certain distance from lives that were obviously ending and which came to threaten discomfort and diminishment more than they promised satisfaction and fulfillment. Hume, of course, had a terminal illness, and Seneca was beginning to lose power and influence in a culture where the individual was much more defined by social roles than in ours. Nonetheless, both exhibited balanced and mature judgment about their prospects in advanced age. The aging individual at least must have something of Hume's and Seneca's readiness for death, if she cannot have Nietzsche's avowed proclivity to practice "the difficult art of leaving at the right time," much less manage his aggressive intention to "convert the stupid physiological fact [of death] into a moral necessity" (Nietzsche, 1967: 484). The readiness for death which Seneca and Hume exhibited is often thought of and described in terms of a *weariness* of life, especially of life that has been less than wholly satisfying, as most unfortunately are. But though fair enough in many cases, this way of thinking about the readiness for death underestimates the degree to which an aged person may understand her prospects, and it lessens the extent to which her decision is realistic and a positive affirmation of her will. But it is difficult for many to conceive of anyone *preferring* to die, so they construe the readiness in question negatively as a kind of despair. Hume's and Seneca's readiness to die is probably difficult to achieve. As indicated, what is required by preemptive suicidal deliberation is somewhat less than their positive readiness for death, namely, a crucial measure of detachment that enables effective suicidal deliberation and enactment.

To conclude this section, and prior to considering a different temporal aspect of preemptive suicide, it will be useful to briefly review the foregoing points. With respect to contravention of interests, the decided-on time for preemptive suicide must be as late as can be judged safe but still within the preemptive-suicide requirement that there be no compelling pressures on the agent. With respect to the coherency of the preference to die, preemptive suicide must be temporally focused in the sense that the reflective aging individual must seriously deliberate preemptive suicide at a particular time, and relative to a specific time of enactment in the present or very near future. Without fulfillment of this requirement, suicidal preference and intention may remain too abstract to involve vivid awareness of consequences. Additionally, the potential preemptive suicidist's deliberation must take place at a time in her life when she is mature enough to appreciate what she is forfeiting in committing suicide. Finally, the potential suicidist must distance herself enough from life to engage in serious and effective deliberation about dying by her own hand. As noted, this last is not actually a temporal condition, but it arises naturally in connection with the agent's maturity. The temporal conditions just summarized do not of themselves provide us with the needed temporal criterion for rational preemptive suicide, but they do determine its character. However, before that criterion can be articulated, a number of other points must be discussed.

Intentional and Material Conditions

The timing of preemptive suicide is a complex matter, having both "material" and "intentional" aspects in the sense that the potential preemptive suicidist must consider not only when her physical condition and prospects most strongly indicate the advisability of preemptive suicide, but also when she feels most ready to end her life. This may initially appear to be exaggeration of the role of values and perceived interests, which would be counter to the qualification to the values criterion I introduced earlier. However, this is not the case. The major reason for the stress on the intentional is that the potential suicidist can never establish with certainty precisely when her suicide would be most efficacious in the sense of being best timed to enable her to live as long as possible with as little risk of personal diminishment as possible. That is, she will not be able to determine the optimum time for her suicide purely on the basis of her material conditions. This inability means that the potential preemptive suicidist, lacking an adequate objective basis for an optimum decision when to end her life, faces the need to *decide* when to die. And her decision will be made more difficult because she must be prepared to relinquish somewhat more of her remaining viable life span than she actually would need to relinquish if her information about the future were complete. To avoid the risk of diminishment and of having her decision to commit preemptive suicide effectively turned into a need to commit surcease suicide, the agent must take her life at a time sooner than is probably necessary. Preemptive suicide is by nature a trade of *some* viable time for the prevention of personal diminishment, and since how much time must be relinquished cannot be determined on the basis of information about material conditions, the potential suicidist's decision must be mainly a product of personal value judgments and assessments of her own circumstances. But in spite of this clarification, there is an obvious tension here with the interests qualification to the values criterion, a tension which dramatically highlights the importance of our discussion in the previous chapter of the reduction of an elderly person's interest in continued life. Without that reduction, preemptive suicide would invariably require highly dubious subjugation of interests to values, and so would possibly never satisfy the qualified values criterion.

Given the pivotal role of values in the preemptive suicidal decision, that decision may well prove impossible to make in many cases. For instance, as suggested in the last section, an elderly person who is enjoying good health and is immersed in her life and relationships, may be more or less psychologically incapable of committing preemptive suicide, because everything in her life will militate against "practic[ing] the difficult art of leaving at the right time." It is just such immersion in life that compounds our biological instincts against taking our own lives. The trouble with "the right time" is that it is always sooner than we would like. I do not mean to trivialize the point with the following analogy, but it is an apt one and often used metaphorically in discussions of suicide. The time to leave a party is prior to the first stifled yawn or the first forced laugh, and that invariably means leaving *before* one is inclined to, since it is exactly the occurrence of such events that incline one to leave. The hard fact is that the right time to leave is before the occurrence of cues that prompt one to leave, and the very hard fact about preemptive suicide is that it means leaving life when the only evident reason for doing so is one's chronological age and its implications. Nor is this fact only a consequence of the need for caution, the need to guard against sudden and devastating misfortune. Since its purpose is to preserve the identity of the agent, preemptive suicide is most appropriate at a time when the agent is most herself, and somewhat paradoxically that means she should take her life while she still has a great deal to lose by doing so. For all of these reasons, then, our consideration of the timing of preemptive suicide has to focus more on the intentional aspect of preemptive suicide than on its material aspect. What needs to be done with respect to the material aspect is relatively straightforward. The potential preemptive suicidist must establish as closely and accurately as possible the nature of her physical state and prospects and what it entails with respect to her mental state and prospects. But once that has been done, the major effort by both the agent and her advisers must be concentrated on judging *her readiness to die*. There simply is no way to establish the correct time for preemptive suicide by reliance on "objective" factors. The agent's readiness to die, then, is crucial, and must be assessed as effectively as possible. Before considering how the agent may best go about assessing her readiness to die, I must clarify a number of points which bear on her assessment.

The Complexities of Timing

The burden rationality imposes on the reflective aging individual choosing to end her life rather than risk personal diminishment is to approximate as closely as possible the moment when she most likely has gotten as much out of life as she can before the danger of diminishment grows too great. But as we saw with respect to the conflict of values and interests generated by the larger role of the intentional in preemptive suicide, this burden comprises somewhat conflicting requirements. The agent must, on the one hand, delay her preemptive suicide as long as possible to minimize the contravention of her interests—though this is not to say she must delay taking her life until she is *certain* of the best time for her suicide. The rationality requirement cannot be that preemptive suicide be an optimized act committed at that one precise moment when the balance of benefit and loss first turns negative with respect to the reflective aging individual's life span. That hypothetical moment not only could never be known, there almost certainly is no such single moment. The rationality requirement can be only that as little viable time be relinquished as is *reasonably* possible, given the limited nature of the information available to the potential suicidist. Nonetheless, the requirement is for the agent to commit suicide as late as she can. On the other hand, the agent must not delay so long that she jeopardizes the soundness of her suicidal deliberation or the point of its enactment. While hasty action would be disastrous—in robbing her of viable time—delay increasingly endangers the rationality of preemptive suicide. There is, then, a real opposition between the demands of rationality as applied to the protection of the agent's interests, and as applied to the requirements of preemptive suicide and the likely effects of the agent's continued existence.

The timing of the agent's suicide is further complicated by the fact that, as discussed in the last section, preemptive suicide is an essentially *discretionary* act. The readiness to die manifested by Seneca and Hume is more than an emotional enhancement of a rational suicidal decision. An attitude which at least approaches that readiness is integral to a rational preemptive suicidal decision. Since she cannot hope to get anywhere by trying to determine the best time for her suicide on the basis of her material conditions, the potential preemptive suicidist must appreciate fully that there is an unavoidable measure of arbitrariness in the timing of preemptive suicide. What she must face is that once the decision to commit preemptive suicide is made, the precise timing of its enactment will involve a degree of spontaneous and intuitive decisiveness within the broader context of adequate grounds for suicide and the reasonably most limited contravention of interests. After the agent has considered all that can be considered with respect to information about her overall health, and heeded the counsel of friends and medical practitioners, the final decision of when to take her life must be based on what she thinks and feels. And though there is more to say about the intentionality of preemptive suicide, what we can say here is that because the preemptive suicidal decision is always underdetermined by the sheer facts of the agent's material situation, it must ultimately turn on the agent's intentional preparedness to quit life.

In the next several sections I shall try to carry the argument forward and simplify things a little by clarifying some points regarding the material conditions of preemptive suicide, introducing the needed temporal criterion to capture the various temporal factors mentioned so far, and considering more carefully—in the context of its temporal aspect—just what preemptive suicide achieves for the agent. I should then be in a position to tackle, in Chapter 7, the still tougher question of the intentional occasion for preemptive suicide.

Sorting Out the Material Context

We can proceed with the question of the timing of preemptive suicide by identifying and excluding a number of possible material conditions which might otherwise confuse the issue. This can be accomplished with a four-way distinction among material conditions in which an elderly person may find herself. First, there is what we can call the "imminent death" condition. This would cover cases where an individual is actually in the process of dying, or is wholly dependent on artificial life-support systems with no hope of improvement, or is in a condition where not even life-support systems can maintain the organism alive as an integrated system capable of sustaining consciousness. The "imminent death" condition is of no interest to us. Once an individual has reached that stage, the question of preemptive suicide is irrelevant, though surcease suicide and euthanasia may still be real options. Second, there is what we can call the "near-death" condition. This is a condition where medical diagnosis predicts death within days or even weeks, and which therefore seems to rule out consideration of preemptive suicide. We can stipulate that where diagnosis indicates death within three months, preemptive suicide is ruled out by the diagnosis itself. Medical prognoses of this scope are now too reliable to accommodate serious enough doubts which would open up conceptual room for preemptive suicide by effectively negating the diagnosis in the mind of the agent. But surcease suicide would remain possible and appropriate. Note that if the diagnosis is that the agent will suffer great pain, the question in any case shifts to the realm of euthanatic or surcease suicide.

The shift just mentioned, though, requires clarification regarding a variety of surcease suicide. The clarification is appropriate here because the situations which most immediately involve the variety in question are "near-death" conditions. It is possible that the diagnosed condition is such that the agent can expect not to suffer until the very end of her truncated life. While preemptive suicide is ruled out, she may nonetheless want to avoid the threatened pain by taking her life prior to its likely onset. Her suicide would then be considered and (possibly) committed in advance of the feared pain or other compelling condition, and so would seem not to be surcease suicide. The only way it would be surcease suicide is if her knowledge of her impending agonizing death constituted an intolerable psychological condition. But the agent might be quite cool about her situation, especially if assured that she will not have to endure the pain in question. This sort of suicide has been in the background of our discussion so far, and it is very likely that it is the sort of suicide most people think of when I have spoken of preemptive suicide. But it is *not* preemptive suicide, since the pressure of the diagnosis is actual and the reason the agent takes her life is to avoid physical pain, not personal diminishment. The point here is that there is what I can only think to call an "anticipatory" version of surcease suicide. An individual may choose to commit suicide on being diagnosed to have a terminal or otherwise devastating condition, but do so before serious symptoms occur—though we can assume enough symptoms have occurred to warrant and support the diagnosis. Her suicide would not be preemptive because of the presence of compelling pressures, but it would not quite be surcease suicide either, since she is not yet in great pain or a similar punishing state and her psychological state is probably not itself sufficiently punishing. Admittedly, the border between preemptive suicide and "anticipatory" surcease suicide is ill-defined and easily crossed. Still, the difference is clear enough in that anticipatory surcease suicide, while not committed when actual conditions are unendurable, is deliberated and committed when those conditions are so reliably anticipated that they exert compelling pressure on the agent. Recall that preemptive suicide, as a trade of *good* time for death on one's own terms, must be deliberated and committed prior to such pressures.

But to return to the point, the third sort of material condition is what we can call the "moribund" condition. Here medical diagnosis is for death after three months but within six months to a year. The "moribund" condition constitutes a gray area. The time in question seems too short for sufficient diminishment to justify preemptive suicide. But aside from questions of physical discomfort, there is the possibility that the psychological implications of the condition may threaten enough personal diminishment to justify preemptive suicide. Against this, the experienced concern and uncertainty may negatively affect preemptive suicidal deliberation, making its rationality problematic. We have here a difficult sort of case which most likely cannot be dealt with in a general way. That is, it will almost certainly prove necessary to consider these cases individually. One would have to examine the agent's attitudes, gauge the degree to which the diagnosis may affect deliberation, and especially assess whether the diagnosis may itself contribute to diminishment of the agent. As in some "near-death" cases, we may find in "moribund" cases that the most appropriate sort of suicide is anticipatory surcease suicide. But to proceed, these cases are also best excluded from our consideration, so that we can concentrate on those more central ones wherein the reflective aging individual considers preemptive suicide in a time frame defined by reasonable expectation that she will live, say, at least another year. The fourth material condition is one where the reflective aging individual is diagnosed as having a fatal but slowly progressive disease which will take her life in two to five years. Preemptive suicide is possible here because the life span projected by the diagnosis does not differ enough to the agent, or possibly in fact, from what she might otherwise anticipate. It could be that the diagnosis itself constitutes a suicidal pressure sufficient to prompt anticipatory surcease suicide, but it is more likely that the period involved is too long to cause the agent that sort of distress. Again, a diagnosis of that sort allows for the sort of hope that would also make anticipatory surcease suicide inappropriate. Moreover, while a period of two to five years may seem a fairly short time to someone in middle age, it can be a large percentage of an aging individual's remaining life span, and the period certainly allows scope for serious personal diminishment. Preemptive suicide could be appropriate, then, regardless of the terminal prognosis. With respect to material conditions, then, we can adopt a pragmatic stance and more or less arbitrarily take one year as marking the difference between clear and not-so-clear cases of preemptive suicide, and accept cases involving shorter periods as requiring consideration on an individual basis. Where the time is short *enough*, or where pressures making surcease suicide appropriate are already operant, the question of preemptive suicide will not arise. In this connection, one thing the proposed temporal criterion should do is enable us to more easily distinguish between preemptive and anticipatory surcease suicide.

The Temporal Criterion

It will be obvious by now that the main reason I am having to add qualifications and new criteria to the criteria for rational suicide is that the criteria as initially set out are primarily designed to cover surcease suicide. Choron and Narveson may imply a fair bit about what I have dubbed preemptive suicide, but most of what they have to say is really about surcease suicide. Battin is exceptional in considering preemptive suicide to some extent, though of course she does not call it that. Even as I reassembled and articulated the various criteria for rational suicide, they were not well suited to preemptive suicide. The need for the interests qualification to the values criterion showed that, because while crucial to preemptive suicide, the qualification is largely immaterial to surcease suicide. The latter does not raise questions about the possible tension between values and perceived interests on the one hand, and real interests on the other, since the individual's real interest in continued life is negated or overridden by unbearable pain, a terminal condition, or a terrible moral dilemma. The addition of the interests qualification to the values criterion was a first step toward refashioning the rationality criteria to serve the assessment of preemptive suicide. Now I need to make criterially explicit the temporal requirement for rational suicide. I also need to amend the criteria to reflect the intentional factors mentioned earlier, namely, mature and adequately detached deliberation and judgment. While the first of these latter is a temporal consideration, and the second arose in connection with temporal considerations, they do not easily fit into the temporal criterion. On the other hand, they seem not to require introduction of still another criterion, because they seem to be implicitly covered by the first or nonimpairment criterion. That is, lack of maturity or insufficiently detached judgment constitute impairment of rational suicidal deliberation. What is needed is simply to change the first criterion to explicitly include reference to maturity and detachment—or better, to exclude immature and insufficiently detached judgment. And in connection with the matter of detached judgment, I shall also add a qualification to the nonimpairment criterion to exclude doxastic compulsion—i.e., undue pressure on the agent due to the force of rigidly held and domineering beliefs. This is the sort of compulsion which was no doubt at work in the Jonestown case, but note that this sort of compulsion is quite different from psychological compulsion due to obsession—something too often overlooked. Doxastic or cognitive compulsion does not distort reasoning, only its premises; psychological compulsion is less discriminating and may distort both. For instance, a South African genuinely convinced that whites are superior to blacks may be capable of exemplary reasoning on the basis of that premise in spite of its falseness. On the other hand, a paranoiac may twist and reshape both premises and reasoning to yield obsessive conclusions about persecution. But to move on, we can amend and reorder the elements in the first criterion, and slightly rephrase other criteria, as follows: To be rational, preemptive suicide must

1. result from deliberation which is consistent with accepted canons of discursive thought and is unimpaired by

reasoning errors, doxastic or psychological compulsion, false beliefs, immature and/or inadequately detached judgment, or lack of relevant information.

2. be based on reasoning about and interpretation of values which are accessible to others than the potential suicidist.

3. be consistent with the agent's operant, well-grounded values, without that consistency being gained by undue depreciation of the agent's interest in continued existence.

4. be in the interests of the agent, at least not harming the agent more than continuing to live would do.

I can now begin to hammer out the required temporal criterion by restating the temporal-focus requirement already considered: given that a reflective aging individual prefers to die rather than be diminished by age, her preference must at some point in her life be actualized at least to the extent that she seriously considers taking her life at that time or in the immediate future. This requirement is not that she actually take her own life at that time, or even that she decide to do so, only that her general preference *poses a real question* at some particular time as opposed to remaining an indeterminately future possibility or even an empty or self-delusory notion. The trouble here is that a good deal remains to be said about how preemptive suicide does come to pose a real question. That is, requirement of temporal specificity of the sort at issue will be insufficient unless I can say how and when preemptive suicide constitutes an actual and pressing option. This matter is complicated and I have devoted all of the next chapter to its discussion. Nonetheless, after articulating the temporal criterion, it will be necessary to say something in this chapter about how preemptive suicide is at least abstractly occasioned by the nature of what preemptive suicide is intended to achieve. But to progress we need at least a working articulation of the temporal criterion. Given what has been said, I will frame the temporal criterion in this way: assuming satisfaction of the amended nonimpairment, accessibility, values, and interests criteria to be rational, preemptive suicide must

5. be considered at a specific time, and sufficiently prior to imminent or actual deterioration for suicide to be unforced forfeiture of remaining life to avoid personal diminishment.

This criterion has several features that make it different from the others and require special note: first, the criterion applies exclusively to preemptive suicide; second, unlike the other criteria, this one specifies the objective of suicide. This specification is necessary because preemptive suicide is not suicide committed as a response to punishing conditions which themselves furnish the requisite objective, namely, their own nullification. To be rational, preemptive suicide's objective must be preventative as opposed to corrective. The specification of preemptive suicide's objective as avoidance of personal diminishment also means that though preemptive, the suicide must have adequate grounds—such as significantly advanced age. Suicide by a forty-year-old individual having no reason to think she is under any degenerative threat would not be rational as a case of *preemptive* suicide. Furthermore, there is an implicit condition in the temporal criterion that if suicide would *not* preserve the agent from diminishment—for example, if there is evidence that significant deterioration has already taken place—it would not be rational as an instance of preemptive suicide, though it might be acceptably rational as surcease suicide.

The Crucial Conditional

To return to the question of the potential suicidist's assessment of her readiness to die, and the actual timing of preemptive suicide, a little more progress can be made by clarifying how, given a preference for death over diminishment, the reflective aging individual may best proceed. In assessing whether the time has come to perhaps enact her preference, she should ask herself when she *would* commit suicide if possessed of the relevant information and having taken into account her desires for whatever future she might have (Brandt, 1975). In other words, she must review the data available to her and what she still hopes to accomplish at her age. She must then judge when she would take her own life if she knew she had all the information pertinent to her decision, and she was prepared to forgo whatever plans she might still have. The agent will likely have to engage in this conditional deliberation more than once, but what she can establish in this way is when she has the *least* possible amount of ambivalence toward taking her own life (Motto, 1972). The strategy here is to shift the focus of the agent's suicidal deliberation and decision from when she *should* commit suicide to why she should *not* do so when the option presents itself forcefully in the context of realization that she has reached an age when her health and mental state are growing precarious. This shift of focus relies on suicide presenting itself as a real option, and its doing so could drastically change the reflective aging individual's situation. As is often true with intentions of great consequence, it may be that when the reflective aging individual acknowledges that there is no good reason to postpone her suicide, she will change her mind or realize that her preference to die is not a real or deep one. The pressing reality of impending enactment of an earlier abstract decision to die may result in the realization that she does not want to end her own life, either because she lacks the courage to do so or because she is willing to risk whatever the future offers. This is the grain of wisdom in Judge Wachtler's remarks about the dangerously routine nature of some avowals of a preference for death over dependency on life-support systems. There is, in any case, no question of compulsion with respect to preemptive suicide. Even if a moment were known to actually be the best for the abandonment of her life, the potential suicidist is completely free to decide to live out her term. As Beeman correctly claims, some individuals may be hopeful enough to sacrifice a good deal of their intellectuality to experience a new, albeit reduced, side of life. In deciding to live on in spite of diminishment, the reflective aging individual would have to understand that the value which might accrue to her in those reduced circumstance would be value only to herself as changed by those circumstances. However, it was Beeman's point that an agent's present assessment of who she will be and what she will value in her altered future state is deeply problematic.

The key factor in deciding whether to commit, postpone, or forgo preemptive suicide is the measure of deteriorative change which the reflective aging individual is willing to risk. The assessment the reflective aging individual must make, then, is how much she is likely to change in continuing to live, and how much of that change she will risk or possibly accept. The resources available for this task are surprisingly rich, though admittedly neither singly nor jointly sufficient to themselves conclusively resolve the issue. These resources include medical and other technical information about how advanced age affects human beings; family histories; personal observation, both of others and of inclinations in oneself; and literary material. A fictive work like *The Stone Angel* (Laurence, 1964) may prove as useful as any set of statistics or the most complete family history by providing a vicarious experience which may play a decisive role in suicidal deliberation. Perhaps the most important resource will be information on how close relatives, especially parents and grandparents, fared in old age. In assessing her situation, the reflective aging individual should imagine herself in the place of her least-favored close relative at a comparable age, asking herself if as that person she would have preferred to die at an earlier time. This is the sort of thing the reflective aging individual must do to determine when she is most ready to die. But the question I face here is how the reflective aging individual is first prompted to begin her suicidal deliberation. The temporal criterion requires that this deliberation be undertaken by the reflective aging individual while she is still undiminished. However, that means, as was noted above, chronological age itself is the only objective determinant of when suicidal deliberation is appropriate. And clearly it is by itself insufficient. There will be catalytic factors, such as pointed awareness of the illnesses or deaths of friends, which will actualize the deliberation chronological age only occasions, but while all of this may be clear enough, something is missing. What makes the foregoing sound oddly unreal is that it misses whatever intentional factor actually moves the reflective aging individual to initiate suicidal deliberation. I have spoken of fear of personal diminishment and loss of identity, but those notions remain too abstract. Given an equation containing awareness of

chronological age and likely consequences, addition of fear of
diminishment or loss of identity does not quite yield the right
sum. We need to better understand how suicide suddenly looks
like a *solution* to something. In pursuing the matter of timing, then,
we again confront the central question of suicide's intentional
objective, of precisely what it is that preemptive suicide achieves
for the agent.

Timing and Identity

The question of *when* preemptive suicide should be done is not
separable from the question of *what* such suicide is supposed to
do. We cannot determine the best time for preemptive suicide or
understand when it becomes a real option without understanding
what it is intended to gain for the agent. Comparison with
surcease suicide is again enlightening. What surcease suicide
does is protect the agent from pointless distress: from distress
which will not be relieved for anything like a significant period
of time, and which cannot be adequately compensated for by
other experience. And here we should understand "distress"
to encompass psychological and other sorts of hardship other
than purely physical agony. This includes the anguish caused
by an inescapable ethical dilemma, since surcease suicide may
also be the only way an agent can escape performing a grossly
immoral act. In both the pain and moral-danger cases, the timing
of surcease suicide is not at issue, for the whole point of such
suicide is to enable the agent to escape something that already
characterizes her existence in a maximally exigent way. The
objective of surcease suicide is evident and unproblematic:
cessation of the conditions that prompt it. If a condition has been
identified but its effects are not yet realized, or at least not yet
discernible, the suicidal objective would be as clear: prevention
of that realization. Anticipatory surcease suicide is suicide
considered and committed when unacceptable or unendurable
circumstances are diagnosed or otherwise soundly anticipated
as imminent. But the timing of anticipatory surcease suicide
is not at issue either, because also determined by a material
condition. There may be some question of precisely when the
agent is best advised to take her life, or she might wait until the

feared effects of her condition begin to be discernible, but these are secondary practical details. The point is that both surcease and anticipatory surcease suicide contrast with preemptive suicide because, in the case of the latter, the only material condition playing a determining role is the agent's chronological age. Preemptive suicide's timing is an *intentional* matter; it is a function of how the reflective aging individual perceives and assesses her situation. Preemptive suicide precisely preempts the possibility of diminishment which anticipatory surcease suicide can only marginally avoid and surcease suicide only escape. The decision to commit preemptive suicide is, as has been stressed, a matter of making a trade: trading *viable* time for certainty that one will not become less than the person who is the sum and product of her history at the time of deliberation and self-inflicted death. The timing of preemptive suicide must *guarantee* the identity of the agent will not be deterioratively affected by age-related factors, whether mental, physical, or a combination of both. This is why the reflective aging individual cannot simply rely on anticipatory surcease suicide; she cannot just wait until there is a specific medical or similar prognosis to occasion deliberation and commission of anticipatory suicide. She cannot count on being lucky enough to have adequate warning of deterioration and enough time in which to deliberate while still free of impairment or seriously intrusive concern about such impairment. The fragility of what preemptive suicide protects, the intentional identity of the agent, rigorously constrains the timing of preemptive suicide.

In Chapter 1 I discussed briefly the requirement that preemptive suicide have an intelligible objective: that we be able to say what it is personal annihilation accomplishes for the agent, beyond the agent's cessation as a subject of experience. And throughout the foregoing chapters I have spoken of the preservation of the agent's identity from deteriorative changes that in effect alter who the agent is. Our identities consist of integrated complex patterns of interwoven memories, attitudes, hopes, and values—though this brief list could be expanded in various ways depending on what terminology we prefer and what aspects of our intentional being we might choose to emphasize. But basically, being *me* at the present time involves who I remember being, and what I remember happening (Parfit, 1971; Prado, 1985); how I view myself and the world around me; what I wish for; and what I prize. We could add what I fear as another defining dimension of self, but perhaps the four mentioned suffice. Age makes a difference to who and what I am in that deterioration of a mental, psychological, or physiological sort negatively affects the individual dimensions of self as well as their integration. Most notoriously, memory is the first to be affected: distant memories are problematically enhanced and embellished, while more recent ones fade and run together, so that the person those memories constitute is subtly—or radically—different from who she was earlier. Attitudes, hopes, and values change too, usually becoming more pronounced and rigid, and so contributing to the altering of the person. And we are largely unaware of these changes because they make us into different people while making it seem that others and the world have changed. In the main age shrinks us. We become more self-centered, we tend to concern ourselves more with the small, even the trivial. We lose interest in what does not directly affect us, we become less resilient to change and novelty. Obviously these changes are not wholly inevitable, nor do they occur in everyone to the same degree, but at the very least they are evident and serious in enough older people around us to support the belief that similar changes will quite likely occur in us. If we think of an individual's intellectual career as progress toward an ideal of self-knowledge and perspicacious awareness (Rorty, 1989: 23–43), it seems fairly clear that at some point age slows that progress and soon begins to reverse it. Age-related changes are the subject of much contemporary discussion (Thorton and Winkler, 1988). Some think them exaggerated or even wholly products of cultural factors, others acknowledge them only with euphemistic technical descriptions like "decreased adaptiveness" or "disengagement." But it is extremely difficult to maintain that age does not blinker and slow us mentally as it dulls our perceptual abilities and checks our readiness of movement. Preemptive suicide is primarily intended to end the individual's career before the slowing and reversal of her progress, where that slowing and reversal really amount to an undoing of the person. Preemptive suicide is designed to achieve protection of the individual, even at the cost of her death. In this way it is analogous to suicide committed for the protection of moral integrity. Its rationale, simply put, is that it is better to die *as oneself* than to live as a lesser version of oneself. But while it may be possible for a person of potent intellectual ability, and possessed of Socratic self-knowledge, to decide, purely on the basis of cool reflection, "This is the best I can be; I choose to die now," most of us—if capable of preemptive suicide at all—will require more pointed prompting. In the next chapter I will consider the nature of that prompting. What has emerged here is that at least part of what was missing from our equation, the elusive central determinant in the timing of preemptive suicidal deliberation, must be forceful recognition that one's identity has been jeopardized by how long one has lived and the nature of human survival.

However, the primary topic of this chapter was timing, and I should briefly recapitulate the main points considered. First, we now have some appreciation of how temporal requirements for rational preemptive suicide are at odds with themselves, necessitating delay for the sake of interests, and its opposite for the sake of rationality and safety. And assuming that most of Chapter 5 was correct, we also appreciate how this opposition is theoretically resolved, at least to a point, by the reduced nature in old age of the interest in continued life. Second, we understand how coherency requires that preemptive suicidal deliberation be temporally focused. Third, we are aware of the dominance of the intentional and discretionary elements of preemptive suicidal deliberation and enactment. Additionally, a little was said about the nature of that deliberation. Fourth, we have a temporal criterion, and small but important amendments to the other criteria for rational suicide, all of which adapt the criteria to the case of preemptive suicide. Fifth, we have considered how the potential preemptive suicidist might best determine her readiness to die. And sixth, we have a better idea of what preemptive suicide achieves and the nature of what it protects. Finally, we have raised in a preliminary way the question of how preemptive suicide presents itself to an agent as a relevant and immediate option. In the next chapter I must pursue this somewhat murkier question.

7

A JAMESIAN LIVE OPTION

> One can never be wretched,
> Who is prepared to die.
>
> Seneca, *Hercules Oetaeus*

It would be very difficult to continue my treatment of preemptive suicide if I had to argue convincingly that the motivation for such suicide must be exclusively rational: that the potential preemptive suicidist must reach and enact her suicidal decision purely on the basis of reasoning yielding the conclusion that she is best advised to take her own life. In this view, preemptive suicidal deliberation, decision, and enactment would constitute an Aristotelian practical syllogism, with abstract acknowledgement of the preferability of death to personal diminishment as the major premise, acceptance of oneself as in danger of personal diminishment because of advanced age as the minor premise, and the suicidal act as the conclusion. In this extreme rationalist construal of preemptive suicide, values would play their chief part only in determining in an abstract way that it is more utile to take one's own life than to endure erosion of identity. What would then be required is the agent's admission that she is under threat of personal diminishment. The agent's subsumption of her own situation under the major premise would be enough to bring about her suicide. But there is something bizarre about an individual deciding to commit suicide, and then doing so, because of a logical exercise in which, having admitted a standing condition, she further admits that it applies to her and as a result takes her own life. What gives Kallimachos's epigram about Kleombrotos its bite is precisely the strangeness of this idea that purely rational considerations—even with Platonic credentials—could suffice for someone to throw himself "down to Hades from a high wall." (Kleombrotos actually drowned himself, but it may have been from a high wall.) Whether of the preemptive, anticipatory surcease, or surcease sort, suicide would appear paradoxically *irr*ational if prompted only by rational factors. The most there could be to the overly rationalistic construal is that, as we saw in Chapter 4, some things can be in one's interests in a "potential benefit" sense that involves recognition of their desirability with no actual desire for them on the part of the agent. Reason could present suicide as just such a potential benefit in the sense of "recommending" it in certain circumstances, as Narveson might put it. But reason cannot make suicide a *compelling* option, much less make it preferred by the agent. Aside from raising complex questions about moving from "is" to "ought" judgments in reaching a conclusion, rational recommendation of suicide must assume that the positive and negative factors considered in assessment of an individual's situation have stable and determinate values. But when what is at stake is the agent's very life, the assessment of positive and negative factors cannot be straightforward, for the magnitude of what is at stake will constantly influence both assessment and factors assessed, invariably weakening the force of negative factors as the prospect of death increases in proximity. There just is no adequate basis for a purely rational judgment that one should commit suicide, because none of the relevant factors are sufficiently determinate or persist unchanged by assessment when the object of the exercise is possible self-annihilation. Even if an individual already has an abstract preference for death over personal diminishment or other overwhelming misfortune, the awesomeness of the act of deliberately terminating one's own life, and instinctive resistance to it, will make what seems intolerable and demanding of death in abstraction seem considerably more benign in the event. A purely rational judgment about the suitability of suicide may evaporate the moment the dreaded situation is viewed from a closer perspective. As Hume would assure us, reason alone cannot move an agent, much less move her to end her life. For an agent to come to have Seneca's willing preparedness to die rather than be wretched, suicide must present itself as what William James—speaking of religious belief—called a "live option" (James, 1956: 9, 11). Suicide must be an option that is immediate and pressing in the sense that there is a strongly felt need to choose or reject the option, as opposed to only intellectual recognition that it is a possible or even advisable course of action. The agent must see suicide as acutely pertinent to her own situation and vying closely with the other alternatives open to her. And the requirement that the choice be real is not only prerequisite for the unqualified possibility of self-inflicted death; it is also a prime requirement for the possibility of *rational* suicide. In requiring complete understanding and knowing decision, rational suicide effectively requires that self-inflicted death be genuinely opted for, rather than fatalistically, uncritically, or obsessively embraced as the "right thing to do" in spite of it being wholly at odds with emotional and other legitimate deliberative elements. It is just this point that most sharply distinguishes rational from non- or irrational suicide, for in the latter cases the agent does not really choose to die; she acts without full awareness and deliberateness because she is confused or driven. We are not *only* rational entities, nor is life a matter of straightforwardly quantifiable pluses and minuses or probabilities which can be weighed one against the other. There is no mere *argument* which will yield a thumbs-up or thumbs-down with respect to the commission of suicide.

The trouble posed by the foregoing with respect to preemptive suicide is that while in the case of surcease and anticipatory surcease suicide the presentation of suicide as an option is forced on the agent in adequately compelling ways—ways which actually tend to eclipse reason—there are no similar unendurable pressures in preemptive suicide. So it seems the presentation of preemptive suicide can only be of a purely rational sort, and so inadequate to prompt acceptable suicidal deliberation and decision. If the onset of diminishment is still only anticipated, it is at least very unclear what does or can turn awareness of preemptive suicide as a rational option—or even an abstract preference for death over diminishment—into a real option, much less an actual preference for death. However,

the likely expectation that what is needed over and above
rational considerations must be sufficiently strong vicarious
or anticipatory distress only blurs the important differences
between preemptive and surcease suicides. I cannot require that
the agent be tormented to consider and decide on preemptive
suicide, because preemptive suicide is precisely not a driven
act. What, then, is it that complements and completes rational
considerations recommending preemptive suicide? The obvious
answer is: motivating values. That is, for preemptive suicide to
present itself as a Jamesian live option, let alone be opted for,
values must qualify the importance of survival and subjugate
it to a kind of life the unattainability of which makes death
actually preferable to continued existence in some other mode.
To be capable of seeing suicide as a real option the agent must
value living only in certain broadly specifiable ways, and strongly
eschew the possibility of living in other ways. Suicide is, after all,
expression of the ultimate negative evaluation of a mode of life
forced on an agent by circumstances. But while it is true enough
that it is motivating values that turn the mere availability of
preemptive suicide as a rational alternative into a Jamesian
live option, and so a potential course of action, the point needs
careful articulation if we are to avoid vitiating the "balance"
or interests-qualification to the value criterion. We cannot now
simply say that what turns the purely rational availability of
suicide into a real option is motivating values. That would
be to allow operant values too dominant a role and either to
turn our discussion of the rationality of preemptive suicide
into a redundant theoretical embellishment of psychological
description, or to accept the relativistic view that suicide is
"rational" if it is merely consistent with the agent's values and
perceived interests. But as we have just seen in the preceding
chapter, recognized danger of personal diminishment seems of
itself insufficient. We need to understand how awareness of, and
possible abstract preference for, rationally justified suicide may
become a pressing choice. While I cannot hope to describe here
how even a Jamesian live option actually becomes an action-
prompting preference for suicide, I can attempt to say how an
agent comes to be faced with a live option. In particular, I shall
try to describe a paradigmatic evaluative element and its role

in the production of a real suicidal option. This is not to say I will offer a psychological theory about preemptive suicidal motivation, but I do need to offer a plausible account of at least what *sort* of additional factor, when added to perception of possible diminishment and the abstract preemptive-suicide option, may suffice to present the agent with a Jamesian live option—and so at least the beginning of an actual preference for elective death.

A Precondition

Conventional wisdom is mostly right in holding that some people are capable of suicide and others are not—or are at most capable of using the threat of suicide or attempts at it as emotional ploys. But conventional wisdom is mostly wrong in thinking the ability is a matter of courage. The greatest likelihood is that, for most, an unthinking acceptance of survival as the absolute value entails unreflective readiness to endure virtually any condition to insure continuance of life. Death is thus put outside the realm of the elective, and rendered an event that must befall one, something that can only *happen*. To most people, therefore, suicide is only an abstraction or at most a distant reality; it is something that other people occasionally do, not something they might do. Often this attitude is a more or less conscious one, due to religious beliefs and training, and is articulated—if at all—in religious terms. But the attitude is more likely due to so deep and unthinking a commitment to personal survival that the thought of voluntary forfeiture of life is alien and repugnant. Nor does the reflective person automatically escape the grip of the attitude in question merely in being reflective, for the roots of the attitude are as deep as our biological nature. How, then, might a person come to see the forfeiture of life as a real and possibly advisable, if not attractive, course of action? Clearly a first step in that process is for the agent to break out of the unthinking commitment to survival just described. The most common way that may happen is that her own survival comes to be *objectified* for her because something threatens its character or, less likely, threatens survival itself. Awareness of danger of significant negative changes to life's familiar mode, to say nothing of danger to the continuation of life, prompts recognition of the vulnerability and precariousness of one's existence. And that recognition forces one's very existence to be pushed to conceptual arm's-length and to be considered as something that transpires in a certain fashion, and which may cease to do so, or may cease altogether. Once existence is recognized as something possessed of certain characteristics, it will immediately be seen that those characteristics could be lost and existence continue. There is then further recognition that worthwhile life and bare survival are different things. The realization that the character of one's life may change radically, that life may continue but be stripped of much or all of what has previously been accepted as normal and knowingly or unknowingly prized, is prerequisite to consideration of suicide. It is so because that realization enables an individual to engage in a minimal but crucial measure of serious reflection on the possible inadequacy of sheer survival. To be receptive to suicide as a real option, an individual must to some degree consider survival as desirable only if it includes features deemed indispensable, such as dignity, independence, adequate gratification, minimal comfort, or retention of her intellectual capacities. To consider suicide a real option, the individual must be sophisticated enough to understand that life is not mere continuance, but is continued existence characterized by a number of essential properties. Anticipatory surcease, surcease, or preemptive suicide will be a Jamesian live option only for an agent who views her life as categorically requiring a number of particular characteristics. And many or even most of those characteristics will be functions of what she prizes, not of what is absolutely necessary for her bare survival as an organism. In short, to seriously consider suicide of whatever sort, the individual must be one who values living her life *as a certain person*, and values that life *as of a certain kind*. As for the actual decision to commit suicide, and enactment of that decision, it is necessary that the individual value her qualified life *enough*—and disvalue alternatives enough—that she prefers to end that life rather than to let it continue under abhorrent conditions.

What we have to understand is how death comes to be a pressing elective issue for an agent, and it seems that for this to happen the agent must first consider that there are modes of life which she would be unwilling to accept for the sake of continued existence. What this consideration does is that by contrasting existence of one sort with another, it not only forces realization that certain sorts of existence are either not worth having or are impossibly repugnant, but by doing so it focuses attention on existence itself as an object of possible choice. But the consideration in question must be of a certain depth. Most people have at one time or another fleetingly thought they would rather be dead than alive in disastrous circumstances, such as surviving an accident as a quadriplegic or having to live as a brutally abused slave. Nonetheless, the huge majority of those who have given a thought to dying over living in such circumstances would in fact accept the circumstances rather than take their own lives. Avowals of preferring death to life under certain conditions are often, as Judge Wachtler reminded us, merely routine or conventional expressions lacking commitment. (Though all New Hampshire drivers proclaim "Live Free or Die" on their license plates, I doubt one in a thousand would live up to their state-imposed slogan.) But assuming consideration of the possible desirability of death over blighted life to be of adequate depth, we can tentatively say at this juncture that a precondition of preemptive suicide being a Jamesian live option is a minimal measure of reflection on the fact that sheer survival is not an absolute value. What must be grasped by the agent is that given who a person is and what she prizes, continued existence lacking certain characteristics and/or possessed of certain others, may not offer adequate compensation for the negative conditions which must be endured. And what is important here is not that the characteristics in question be specified or even be very clear; rather it is that the agent come to think of life, of existence, as something amenable to assessment of whether or not it is worthwhile. Coming to think of life in terms of a need for a positive overall ratio of good to bad is enough to distance an extant individual from her existence sufficiently to enable consideration of whether survival is desirable or even tolerable under certain conditions. However, even if an individual achieves the necessary distance from her own existence to think effectively about whether or not it offers adequate positive content, and so stops thinking of survival as *in itself* adequate, this preconditional state of mind may vary greatly. It may range from vivid but still abstract recognition that life might not be worth living in various circumstances, to compelling awareness that her *own* life would not be worth living in specific circumstances. This range of possibilities highlights the need to get clear on what is operant in moving an agent from the former to the latter sort of awareness, and then from awareness that her own life would not be worth living in the circumstances she dreads, to preferring to die in those circumstances. As noted, we are not here looking for specific psychological motivating factors, which would apply only to particular individuals, nor trying to develop a theory of suicidal motivation, but we do need to identify the sort of evaluative element which, when added to the abstract realization that life may come to be not worth living, prompts an agent to soberly consider that *her* life may be better ended.

Fittingness

The case of the general is again useful. The general faces a situation similar in some important respects to that of the reflective aging individual who is aware of preemptive suicide as a rational option. The general can be assumed to have abstract understanding that his samurai code requires his life in the event of important failure on his part. But it is not until that failure occurs that the general has to deal with the requirement as it applies to his own life. At that time, the requirement could remain an abstraction, or it could become a Jamesian live option, and what makes the difference in the general's case may be very like what makes the difference in the reflective aging individual's case. It is possible that a Japanese officer might continue to understand the samurai-code requirement, but not see it as a Jamesian live option with respect to his own case. (To my knowledge, Japan had no women officers during World War II.) This might be due to bad faith or a superficial commitment to the code, but it could be due to genuine conviction that either the code must no longer be taken literally or that it does not apply in the relevant respect to his situation. The point is, though, that something more is needed than that the officer know the code and its requirements, and share the values it embodies, for him to seriously set about committing *sepuku*. However, the general does move from abstract understanding and endorsement to particular onus; he does come to judge that his life is forfeit.

I want to suggest that the way he arrives at that judgment involves the role of an evaluative element which positively enhances his perception of his own death by ritual suicide. But this is not to say that death by his own hand loses its awful force; it is not rendered somehow more palatable by the general's values. For one thing, we have ruled out that death could be made desirable by false beliefs—for instance to the effect that it is only a transitional entry into some heaven. Nonetheless, the general's evaluative perception of his own self-inflicted death is one which, though it cannot render that death appealing, does confer on it a *meaningfulness* it would otherwise lack. The key to understanding the importance of the positive evaluative perception the general has of his own death is appreciation that, ideally, *sepuku* is not a way of avoiding disgrace or retribution; it is not a way of escaping a hopeless predicament or even predominately of atoning for mistakes. The point of the suicidal demand made by *bushido* or the samurai code is not just to exact atonement, provide release, or inflict punishment. For a true samurai *sepuku* would be the *best* and *most fitting* way to end a life which, unfortunately, came to be characterized by significant failure and hence loss of personal honor. The general must eventually die, and *sepuku* offers him the opportunity to precipitate the inevitable in a way that makes death add meaning to his life rather than being an event that simply ends that life. In committing *sepuku* the general manifests his own rejection of his failures and his unwillingness to live as someone who has been shown incompetent. In committing *sepuku* the general confirms everything that he has lived for and which he has valued, as well as redeeming what he has lost. He is not, as Westerners would think, only paying with his life for a serious transgression. The general does atone for his failures in taking his own life, but what he primarily does in dying by his own hand is meet standards he could not achieve in life. But beyond the samurai code and the culture in which it is embedded, the key point is that the general, in committing suicide, takes his death out of the realm of the merely occurrent and makes it an intentional, value-dictated act. (Recall Nietzsche's remark about turning death into a moral necessity, Nietzsche, 1967: 484.) The general appropriates his own death and enables it to bear a significance it would not have as a caused event. However, what is crucial to our concerns is less that the general achieves what he does than that he perceives his suicide as the means of giving his death special meaningfulness. He sees *sepuku* as the way to make his death satisfaction of a moral demand, rather than allowing it to occur as a caused—albeit later—event.

Whether or not the evaluatory perception the general has of his own death by ritual suicide suffices for him to actually take his own life can remain moot. It is enough for my purpose that in this way suicide does become for him a Jamesian live option. And that it does is evident in the nature of his decision. While we may not agree with his evaluation, we can see that once the general has construed his death as capable of bearing the significance just described, to then reject *sepuku* would not be to simply continue living. Instead it would be to make a deliberate choice against an option which presents itself to him as of real value. The general's perception of *sepuku* as a way of bearing ultimate testimony to what he prizes takes suicide out of the abstract domain and makes it a particular and pressing object of choice. He cannot then refrain from making a choice even by doing nothing. Perception of his possible meaning-imbued death creates an ineradicable contrast with natural (or accidental) death as an inevitable but meaningless event.

The evaluative element operant in presenting suicide as a real option to the general may be equally crucial in making preemptive suicide a real option for the reflective aging individual. The turning of the abstract option of preemptive suicide into a Jamesian live option may be accomplished through perception of *fittingness*. That is, an agent may come to see suicide as an apt end to life: an end which, like the general's *sepuku*, adds significance to an inescapable event which would otherwise occur simply as a caused event. Abstract awareness of the option of preemptive suicide, initiated by rational considerations, may become a particular and real option when self-inflicted death is perceived as not only advisable for preventive reasons, but as having value in itself. That is, given a strongly negative evaluation of inescapable eventual deteriorative changes in herself, and given her understanding that she must in any case die, an agent will further understand that elective death can have not only preventive utility, but a positive value in being a good—perhaps the best—way to end her life. When the awareness of preemptive suicide as a rational option is complemented by perception of suicide as an estimable end to life, then the agent is faced with an actual option, and is some of the way to an actual preference for elective death. There is a close parallel here to someone believing that her death is the most effective way to advance her most cherished life's project, as may be the case in martyrdom (Battin, 1982). But it is crucial to appreciating the role of perception of fittingness, in the presentation of preemptive suicide as a real option, to understand that preemptive suicide is not *primarily* a way of promoting a particular project, much less of getting out of something, as is surcease suicide. Preemptive suicide is considered and committed with a view to preserving one's intellectual identity, and in the evaluative perception preemptive suicide is not only seen as effective in preserving identity from deteriorative influences, but as doing so in a fashion that *enhances* that identity by affirming the values which define it. To return to the party analogy, leaving at the right time is more than a way of avoiding the tedious winding down of the occasion. It is both a compliment to one's host and a proper complement to an enjoyable time, because it is a way of decorously ending what must in any case end. And because it *is* decorous, the act adds value to the experience in spite of being its deliberate termination. This is perhaps the most difficult thing to grasp about preemptive suicide: while it is a forfeiture of remaining life, it adds value to life already lived. What is underemphasized in Seneca and Hume, but is sharply evident in Nietzsche, is the point made above about appropriation of death. Some forms of suicide are an appropriation of one's inevitable death in the sense of making it an act, as opposed to letting it come as an event imposed from outside. Differently put, one makes death an act *in* life rather than letting it be only the end *to* life. Death is both wholly inescapable and as momentous for an individual as her birth, yet it usually comes, as birth always must, as a consequence of external causes. In committing *sepuku* the general transforms what would eventually occur as a final, externally caused event into an assertive act of value endorsement and the fulfillment of a duty. We may not agree with his and his peers' construal and evaluation of his act, and so may argue that it is unduly at odds with the general's basic interest in continued life, but we can appreciate how his perception of his self-inflicted death changes a fated occurrence into a voluntary and portentous enactment of principle. In the same way, the reflective aging individual's perception of her self-inflicted death changes a causal inevitability to a self-protective affirmation of what she most prizes.

There is one important difference to be noted here. The reflective aging individual, unlike the general, does not face the question of suicide because of failures on her part. Her suicidal deliberation does not occur in the context of public judgment of her actions. The question arises because she recognizes, albeit abstractly, that one way to avoid the decline she fears is to deliberately end her own life. The perception of self-inflicted death as acquiring a significance it would otherwise lack, then, is somewhat different for the elderly person than it is for the general. Missing in the case of the reflective aging individual is the additional enhancement provided for the general by public estimation of his suicide. His ritual suicide does not serve only his own interests; it enhances the samurai code and indirectly the culture which supports that code. The general is aware of this, and while personal honor is not changed by public opinion, the respect and esteem his *sepuku* will gain for him cannot be ignored as a factor in his deliberation and decision. Unless her circumstances are very special, the reflective aging individual's appropriation of her own death will not garner public admiration. Her death does not enhance a code or culture other than the basic humanism her values instantiate. Nonetheless, the evaluative perception plays the same basic option-enhancing role for the reflective aging individual that it plays for the general. The noted difference means only that her perception may be somewhat less powerful. But then we must recall Seneca's point that in old age reasons for living are no longer as pressing as they once were. While in the case of the general the public acclaim to be gained by his death may be a potent additional incentive to commit *sepuku*, and so a crucial factor in overcoming a strong inclination to continue living, the absence of that acclaim in the case of the aging individual is matched by her weaker commitment to continued life. Moreover, though the attractiveness of adding public significance to one's death may be missing in the aging individual's case, the awareness of the inevitability of death is greatly heightened, and further compensates for any decrease in the power of the perception of self-inflicted death as fitting. In any case, it must be kept in mind that the enhancing role of perceived fittingness is limited. It is not difficult to think of the idea of perceived fittingness as overly romantic and bound to fail when the agent faces the hard reality of killing herself. But the point is not that the evaluatory perception facilitates *committing* suicide, only that it makes the choice of whether to do so a real and pressing one by imbuing elective death with merit deriving from the agent's own values and priorities. The essential point is that in perceiving her self-inflicted death as fitting in the way suggested, the agent comes to see preemptive suicide as an action in the context of her own needs and intentions, as opposed to only an open possibility. Preemptive suicide ceases to be an abstract solution to hypothetical situations, and becomes the agent's particular response to her own concerns and fears. What the perception of fittingness does is make death cease to be an inevitable, relatively distant fact and become her (potential) immediate, individual act of closure.

I might pull together the foregoing points by saying that awareness of suicide as an option goes through at least three different stages: first, the agent acquires basic understanding that it is possible for her to take her own life; second, the agent acquires further understanding that suicide is both a rational and possibly advisable course of action under certain circumstances; third, the agent may come to see her own suicide as a Jamesian live option. The differences here between preemptive suicide and anticipatory surcease and surcease suicide are that in the case of the latter two, the progression through the three stages is much more rapid because accomplished under great pressure, and it probably involves a higher degree of conviction in the second and particularly in the third stage. In surcease suicide the awareness of suicide as a rational and possibly advisable option is turned into a Jamesian live option not by the agent's own construal of her situation but by external pressures acting on the agent.

In preemptive suicide there are no specific external pressures operant to present suicide as a Jamesian live option, much less to force its choice. The suggestion, then, is that live-option status is achieved by a value-enhanced perception of self-inflicted death, that the move from the second to the third stage of awareness is prompted by the agent's vision of her self-inflicted death as not only resolving her anticipated difficulties, but as providing a significant and fitting end to her life. However, when we compare the evaluative element in question to the sorts of pressures that may prompt surcease suicide, it will likely be difficult to accept that an evaluatory perception can really make the difference between preemptive suicide being an option of which the agent is merely cognizant, and its being a pressing choice for that agent. It will seem to many that an evaluatory perception of this sort must itself be too abstract to make suicide a Jamesian live option. It is important to remember, therefore, that all we require of the perception is that it present preemptive suicide as something about which a decision must be made. The agent's decision could well go against committing suicide; the evaluatory perception is not itself a preference-determining factor. What it does is augment and particularize an abstract option.

It should be said here that even if fittingness still relates to a largely conjectural situation, there is an additional element at work, namely, the temporal aspect considered in Chapter 6. Assuming that the initial interest in suicide is fueled by a serious measure of disquiet over her prospects, the agent's attention is not only focused on her suicide by perception of its fittingness, but also by her understanding that preemptive suicide imposes fairly rigorous timing. If perceived fittingness is insufficient for suicide to be a Jamesian live option, what will complete the transformation is appreciation that preemptive suicide is only possible within certain temporal limits. Given knowledge that age, in raising the matter of preemptive suicide, has already substantially narrowed the temporal possibilities, the agent will see suicide as a pressing option. The perception of fittingness actually entails appreciation of temporal limitations, for the agent will be aware that her suicidal decision and death can only be significant and fitting if that decision is enacted prior to a time when the rationality of her act would become questionable. But for perceived fittingness to play the role described in making preemptive suicide a Jamesian live option, it must be possible for the potential suicidist to rationally prefer a fitting death to continued, albeit uncertain, life. This brings us finally to the question with which we began, namely, whether it is coherent to prefer death to life.

Coherence

Our basic question, postponed until now, is whether or not it is coherent to prefer personal annihilation to life under certain actual or, with respect to preemptive suicide, somewhat distant anticipated conditions. As was suggested before, the matter of coherency is not for us a linguistic or purely logical one of whether the proposition "x prefers to die" or any version thereof is contradictory. The issue is more complex, centering not on literal meaning but on whether someone claiming to have a preference for death has Harman's "vivid awareness" of the annihilatory consequences of suicide. The reason vivid awareness of consequences seems so necessary is that deciding on suicide is choosing to *not exist* because some aspect of existence is judged unsupportable. Moreover, our special interest is in a form of suicide wherein choosing not to exist is not facilitated by pressures which radically devalue existence. This "facilitation" may be suspect with respect to the rationality of even most cases of surcease suicide, since it could be due largely to emotional factors which simply block rational consideration or seriously skew operant values. But unrelieved anguish does reduce the importance of the agent's vivid awareness of the consequences of suicide just to the extent that the agent is in otherwise irremediable torment. In preemptive suicide, though, there is no similar devaluing of life and easing of the requirement; the agent is not under immediate pressure of any sort, and so entirely responsible for her decision and its enactment, and hence she is accountable for fully understanding what she is doing. Preemptive suicide demands special assurance that the agent appreciates the nature of her choice. And the worry that mainly prompts the coherency question is that since we cannot imagine what it is to not exist (Williams, 1973), the agent may not be able to achieve the full appreciation required. The question about coherency, then, might be put in terms of whether it is possible for an agent to rationally want what seems to be beyond her comprehension.

It might be objected that "coherence" is here being misused, and that what is needed is a less logically or cognitively specific and more psychologically descriptive term. However, this is not the case. The root issue is one about coherence because we are concerned with possible contradiction of a sort, since the main question is whether an agent's preference for death is a preference for *death*, as opposed to really being a preference for some other vaguely or confusedly envisaged state. We are dealing with coherence because the question is whether or not a putative preference for death is in some way a preference for *non*death. The most obvious way an apparent preference for death may fail to be a preference for personal annihilation is one I have ruled out, namely, where an individual believes that "physical" death is only a transition to some other level or sort of existence. A less obvious way is for an individual to contemplate or commit suicide with the muddled idea—so prevalent in pathological and near-pathological cases—that she will retain some measure of posthumous awareness, particularly of the emotional effects on others of her suicide. However, I am not primarily concerned with cases where there is some muddled but positive idea about the continuation of personal awareness after death, since in those cases the lack of coherence is evident. What most concerns me is the way an apparently rational preference for death could be rendered incoherent because of a lack of vivid awareness of the nature of personal extinction. And the question of how preemptive suicide becomes a Jamesian live option is closely tied to the question of the coherence of the preference for death, because only if personal annihilation is an intentional object in deliberation can preemptive suicide pose a real option for the agent. Suicide's being a real option is also crucial to the agent's having a coherent preference to die, since it is *actual* preferences that count with respect to preemptive suicide's rationality. Whether or not an abstract preference to die is coherent hardly matters, since its coherence does not suffice to make an agent's actual preference at a particular time also coherent. This is the point we considered in stressing that an abstract preference for death over personal diminishment might well remain abstract and insufficient to prompt earnest consideration of suicide, much less suicidal action. It is the agent's operant, action-determining preference which must be coherent. The agent must truly and coherently prefer to die *in the event*, not prior to it. As we saw earlier, given the nature of elective death, it may well be that some of the agent's real feelings about suicide will emerge only when she is faced with it as an imminent possibility. The implications of suicide might not be fully evident to her until it becomes a Jamesian live option and suicidal action is an immediate prospect. Nor is this to raise in a new way the specter of psychological determinants. It is to admit once more that we are not purely rational creatures, and that we do not always know our own minds about some of our options before they become impending choices. It would be ludicrous, in considering action of the magnitude of deliberate personal annihilation, to reject some decision-influencing factors as merely "emotional" or obviously extraneous because they emerge only under the duress of actually facing the hard choice of whether to live or die. Regardless of its late appearance, each such factor must be duly weighed in the suicidal decision. Some will certainly be dismissible as understandable last-minute fears, but others may be importantly revealing of the agent's state of mind.

The tie between the reality of the suicidal option and the coherence of the preference to die also involves the evaluatory perception of the fittingness of suicide. The perception contributes importantly to the coherence of the preference to die. It does so by giving specific content to the idea of elective death, which would otherwise be only the rather bare notion of the deliberate termination of life. The way the evaluatory perception adds content can be clarified with yet another comparison between surcease and preemptive suicide. The surcease suicidist's judgment is: "Let *this* end, even if everything else must end." The surcease suicidist has a pressing and intolerable intentional object in the condition she wishes desperately to escape, and the nature of that object is so determinate that the main worry is that it may obscure the value of what the suicidist is prepared to relinquish.

But the very nature of this worry indicates that there is no lack of content to the potential surcease suicidist's consideration of elective death. That content is the powerful rejection of, and desire to end, what most fills the agent's awareness. The surcease case is characterized by the actuality and potency of agonizing life, and that actuality and potency give a reflected power and substance to the contemplated alternative, namely, self-inflicted death as the intentional object of suicidal deliberation. They do so by making death more than the difficult-to-conceive cessation of personal existence; they make it a tangible and compelling release from an unendurable condition.

The preemptive suicidist's judgment is quite different from that of the surcease suicidist. Her judgment is: "Better that everything end now, than I be diminished in myself," where diminishment is still a fairly distant eventuality. There can be no ostensive reference comparable to the surcease suicidist's *"this"* in the preemptive suicidist's judgment. In the preemptive case the content and force of what prompts suicidal deliberation is wholly a function of the agent's anticipatory envisagement and consequent evaluation. And the question that haunts the notion of preemptive suicide is whether a disvalued but only envisaged condition can suffice as the counterpoint in an adequate appraisal of the value of present life—a value enriched by the reasonable expectation that life will continue in an acceptable manner for at least some time before it is characterized by personal diminishment.

The worry here is that an anticipated condition is simply not a powerful enough consideration to adequately distance the agent from the life in which she is immersed and to compel full appreciation of what she is doing in committing suicide. Put somewhat differently, the concern is that the power of at-present acceptable life, undiluted by the agony of the surcease case, keeps consideration of death at too abstract a level and prevents the reality of annihilation from figuring properly in the potential suicidist's deliberation. But it is just here that the evaluatory perception of elective death as a fitting end to life functions somewhat as does the punishing condition in surcease suicide. As the punishing condition lends strength and substance to the idea of death by particularizing and substantiating it as escape from anguish, the evaluatory perception particularizes and substantiates preemptive death. What would otherwise be thought of rather starkly as personal extinction, and which would then perhaps not be properly appreciated as to its nature, is given graspable and forceful content when perceived by the potential preemptive suicidist as the consequences of an act which is not only the deliberate ending of her own life for good reasons, but a fitting end to life and an estimable affirmation of value and principle.

Whereas the surcease suicidist gets a grip on the idea of her death by seeing it as release, the preemptive suicidist does so by seeing the extinction of her existence as a decisive act that adds value to the life it finishes. In fact, it is just this perception, but exaggerated and distorted by false belief, that enables martyrs to give their lives for religious and political causes. And the martyr's case is instructive, for it not only shows us the power of the perception in question, it alerts us to the danger that values may take undue precedence over interests. The likeliest form this danger would take is cultural factors so exaggerating the perceived fittingness of death that the interest in continued life is illegitimately overridden. The general's case is again productive, since his samurai code is precisely the kind of value-set likely to be romanticized by his cultural background, and so tends to figure too prominently and decisively in his deliberation. Balancing values and interests clearly is not simply a matter of applying the values and interests criteria. It requires that the agent and her counsellors undertake as objective an assessment as possible of the cultural influences pertinent to her deliberation.

Fortunately, in our time cultural differences are both better recognized and somewhat reduced, so judgment and assessment of the sort required is facilitated. But we have the Jonestown example to remind us of the danger of what I called doxastic compulsion in amending the nonimpairment criterion. In any case, I cannot hope to inventory and deal with possible cultural influences of the sort in question. What is important here is to make clear the pivotal role played by the evaluatory perception in the particularizing and concretizing of elective death as an object of suicidal deliberation. The way this role can be illegitimately decisive and override interests shows the power of the evaluative perception. Once the role of the evaluative perception is appreciated, it becomes reasonably clear that the question whether a potential suicidist has vivid awareness of the annihilatory consequences of suicide is answered to the extent that the agent comes to have her own extinction as the intentional object of her deliberation on a value-driven act of personal closure. If the intent of the potential suicidist is precisely personal annihilation both as a way of eluding diminishment *and* as a final principle-affirming gesture, it would be difficult to sustain doubt that she understood the nature of self-inflicted death.

Coherent by Default?

The question now is whether we have not in fact resolved the coherence issue through attrition. Consider what has been accomplished toward showing preemptive suicide capable of being rational: first, various putatively satisfiable criteria for rational suicide have been formulated; second, the difficult question of how the interests criterion can be met has been shown answerable in terms of the decreased interest in continued existence characteristic of advanced age; third, it has been shown how an evaluatory perception can make suicide a Jamesian live option for an agent; fourth, it has also been shown how the same sort of evaluatory perception may give content to the intentional object of preemptive suicidal deliberation and decision, and thereby facilitate an agent's understanding of the consequences of her suicidal act. We seem able to conclude, then, that it can be rational to preemptively take one's own life in old age. Consider now what it would be to wonder if the agent has a coherent preference for death over and above the criterially established rationality of preemptive suicide. For the *general* question to retain content, it must apply not only to cases that are somehow problematic—for instance where the agent exhibits ambivalence of a worrying sort—but to "best case" instances wherein the nonimpairment and interests criteria are met. What, then, would we be asking with respect to such cases if we press the question about "full," "adequate," or "sufficient" understanding of the consequences of suicide? Would we not be manifesting only "Cartesian Anxiety" (Bernstein, 1987) in asking for conclusive assurance that preemptive suicide not only meets the various requirements but further involves "vivid awareness" of the annihilatory result of self-inflicted death? That is, would we not be manifesting a misconceived Cartesian yearning for a kind of certainty which is unachievable given the limited nature of human intentionality, conception, and imagination? After all, what could it be for an agent truly to have the sort of vivid awareness of the consequences of suicide which the pressed general coherence question seems to require? Would it not be for the potential suicidist *to know what it is like to be dead*? Put in this way the point is clear enough: once we have said all we can about satisfaction of the several criteria for rationality, and about the reality for the agent of the suicidal option, there is no more to be said about the coherency of preferring to die. We cannot be required to describe and identify a single state of mind which is vivid awareness of the consequences of suicide. If the several criteria for rational suicide—and attendant requirements regarding immediacy of the suicidal option—are judged capable of being satisfied, then suicide must be judged capable of being rational. And if these same criteria and requirements are judged to be satisfied with respect to a particular case, then the suicide in question must be judged to be rational. To ask for more, either in terms of one or more of the conditions being irrefutably known to be satisfied, or in terms of conclusive verification of the presence of "vivid awareness" of consequences, would be to demand impossible guarantees that our—and the agents'—judgments about particular suicides are certain and irrevocable in some impossible Cartesian sense. If we can map out how suicide *may* be rational, that must suffice with respect to the general issue, and what remains is a matter of dealing with a lengthy series of empirical questions about individual cases. Admittedly, even the soundest of suicidal decisions can be undermined by some last-minute revelation or emotional or psychological factor, but that is not the sort of possibility that undermines the rationality of suicide generally, so not the sort that interests us. My concern is to show that it is possible for a reflective person of advanced years, who is prompted by realistic evaluation of her prospects and is possessed of a well-grounded evaluatory perception of her death, to make and enact a soundly based and reasoned decision

to end her life. There is no place in this project for misguided
efforts at answering misconceived metaphysical questions about
an agent's chimerically precise state of mind at the time of her
suicidal decision or act.

But it should not be thought that the coherency question
was from the beginning an empty or confused one, or that
it was raised only for strategic reasons. The question arises
genuinely enough, and springs from a realization of the value
and fragility of life and the irreversibility of suicide. The form
the question takes is a deep concern that a potential suicidist
may somehow fail to understand the finality of what her act
entails—which is a very real possibility, and sadly one that is
too often realized. Once raised, the coherency question exhibits
impressive persistence, even to the extent of our thinking that
however sound suicidal deliberation might be, there is still a
possibility that the most sophisticated and meticulous reasoning
on the part of a potential suicidist could fall short of "real"
understanding of the result of her contemplated act. We may
think, for instance, that the very care given to suicidal deliberation
could *itself* vitiate the suicidist's reasoning by making death too
abstract and overly objectified a consideration. We may put our
trust in our instinctive resistance to death and thus devalue
reasoning and argument inclining us toward it. It is just this sort
of response to suicide that we articulate by asking if the agent
can fully comprehend what she is considering. And the more
committed we are to survival, the less ready we will be to accept
that she could have adequate comprehension and still proceed
with her deliberation, much less with actual suicide. There can
be no doubt that the question of coherency is fundamental, for
without adequate understanding of the nature of death, no
amount of deliberation, however sound, could make suicide
rational. However, the fundamentality of the coherency question
may not be in the form of its being a single question needing to
be answered prior to application of the rationality criteria and of
the other requirements considered. It may be that the coherency
question is a complex or "umbrella" one and amenable to being
answered through piecemeal resolution of the issues which the
rationality criteria address, and by clarification of other sorts
of considerations such as how suicide poses a real option to

an agent. If this is the case, there will be nothing left to the coherency question once the individual issues have been dealt with. At the very least, the criterial approach to the rationality of suicide puts the onus regarding queries about coherency where it belongs: on those who would deny us the right to quit life before it destroys us.

A Final Emendation

To close this chapter it is necessary to add a last qualification to the rationality criteria, specifically, to the nonimpairment criterion, to reflect the foregoing discussion. It will also be useful to bring the five criteria together, giving them their final formulation, and to rephrase them somewhat more elegantly and in light of what has been said since their last articulation. It is also important to make explicit here what has been implicit throughout, that the criteria are individually and jointly *necessary*. I would like to say they are also jointly *sufficient*, but that would presuppose resolution of too many empirical questions, and perhaps some conceptual ones. The criteria in their final version, then, are as follows: *Preemptive suicide* is rational when,

1. posing a real option for the agent, it results from mature and adequately detached deliberation consistent with accepted canons of discursive thought, and is unimpaired by reasoning errors, doxastic or psychological compulsion, false beliefs, or lack of relevant information.
2. the deliberation and operant interpretation of values are accessible to others than the suicidist.
3. suicide is consistent with the agent's well-grounded values without undue depreciation of the agent's interest in continued existence.
4. it is in the interests of the agent, not harming the agent more than continuing to live.
5. it is considered at a specific time, sufficiently prior to imminent or actual deterioration to allow an unforced forfeiture of life to avoid soundly anticipated personal diminishment.

8

THE LAST CHOICE

Prudence and courage should engage us to rid ourselves . . . of existence, when it becomes a burden.

Hume, "On Suicide"

My argument for rational preemptive suicide must be a persua-
sive one; there is no possibility of *demonstrating* that preemptive
suicide is rational. Even if one believes philosophical argumentation capable of providing certitude, a number of factors prevent
such demonstration. First of all, whatever may be said generally
about preemptive suicide's rationality, the crucial question will
always be about its instances: about whether particular cases of
preemptive suicide are or are not rational. And while criteria
may be made available which, when met, justify the description
of a case of suicide as rational, that description will be essentially hypothetical because contingent on conscious states
directly accessible solely to the agent, and which are in any
case not wholly determinate due to their intentional nature.
That is, as states of consciousness whose intentional objects
are complex and emotionally charged decisions, evaluations,
and objectives, the states in question lack the definiteness and
stability necessary to be subjects of categorical judgments. The
agent ambivalence inherent in so momentous a decision as that of
self-annihilation must always make problematic any judgments
about that decision, whether made by others or by the agent
herself. Secondly, there will always be significant interpretive
latitude in application and satisfaction of the rationality criteria

in different cases, not only because of the complexity and inexact intentional nature of what they assess, but also because of changes and differences in standards for discursive thought and value priorities. This means that conclusions reached about particular suicides will always be context-dependent and will vary to some degree with time and place. The various criteria for rational preemptive suicide can only delineate what must be the case for something to be an instance of such suicide; they cannot include guarantees of their own consistent and effective application to particular suicides. Therefore, we cannot identify even one wholly unproblematic case of rational preemptive suicide to confirm claims about its rationality. As mentioned before, all that can be done is to show how preemptive suicide is *possible*. Preemptive suicide is a paradigm of those subjects Aristotle warns of, which by their very nature limit the degree of exactness with which they can be treated.

A Practical Definition of Rationality

Basically, the project of showing that the preemptive suicide can be rational is a matter of introducing, or reintroducing, the criterial wherewithal for the practice of judging some cases of suicide instances of a unique form of justified self-inflicted death. And what this comes to is providing a way of categorizing some cases of suicide as instances of a kind of elective death not assimilable to psychologically or otherwise *forced* behavior—whether by the unbearable persecution of persistent pain, the crushing relentlessness of a moral dilemma, or any other effectively irresistible influence on the agent. Provision of the required criteria is necessitated by a cultural conception of suicide which denies us self-inflicted death as a free option—a paradoxical denial, given that it is quite at odds with the same culture's insistence on the priority of personal freedom (Baechler, 1975). The denial is effected by widespread construal of suicide as not rational—as pathological unless compelled by the direst and most immediately pressing circumstances, or, possibly, by the noblest of other-directed motives. Nor are things better at more elevated professional levels, because there suicide is theoretically conceived in mainly causal terms and almost independently of the agent's own intentions and volition. As we shall see in the next section, the rationality of suicide is precluded, or at least unacceptably circumscribed, when suicide is theoretically objectified as the outcome of social or psychological pressures acting on the agent.

Showing preemptive suicide can be rational, however, is not just a matter of providing criteria to distinguish some cases of preemptive suicide from others. Unlike surcease and anticipatory surcease suicide, which can be rational to a greater or lesser degree, preemptive suicide is in fact defined by the rationality I am claiming for it. To be a discrete form of self-inflicted death, preemptive suicide must be the product of sound, coolly reflective deliberation, and of knowing, deliberate enactment. Otherwise, because done in the absence of negative pressures, preemptive suicide would always be counter to interests. The perhaps assumable *fact* of inevitable eventual diminishment is of itself insufficient to justify preemptive suicide. In short, self-inflicted death must satisfy all of the criteria I have considered in order to be rational preemptive suicide; only if there is a mode of self-annihilation which satisfies the criteria listed at the end of Chapter 7 is there such a thing as rational preemptive suicide. If one or another condition is not met, then self-inflicted death, whether realized or only contemplated, will be some other form of suicide, and likely one that is not fully rational.

One advantage to the identity of preemptive suicide with *rational* preemptive suicide is that the proffered criteria and ancillary requirements do considerably more than define the conditions in which self-inflicted death is deemed rationally preemptive. The criteria in effect provide a contextual definition of the relevant form of rationality. The criteria themselves provide the relevant sense of "rational" because, in giving the specifications suicide must meet to be preemptive and rational, their own statement spells out what it means to say that preemptive suicide is rational. But this is not because the criteria pick out something independent of both themselves and their employment and to which preemptive suicide must *conform*. The reality of rational preemptive suicide is wholly intentional, a matter of perception. That is, it is a matter of how it is construed and held to the relevant standards by both the suicidist and her peers. The only brute reality is the death of the agent. Everything else supervenes on that reality. Even the more or less straightforwardly procedural matter of assessing the satisfaction of the nonimpairment criterion is crucially judgmental and interpretive for both the agent and her peers. And the agent's and her peers' appraisals and construals are throughout mutually interdependent. On the one hand, an agent must satisfy the accessibility requirement of the second criterion. On the other hand, an instance of preemptive suicide could be judged rational by a suicidist's peers, and still not be rational from the agent's point of view. To say that a self-inflicted death was "objectively" rational preemptive suicide, even though not thought so by the suicidist herself, would be to utter metaphysical nonsense. An individual who takes her own life while convinced that she is doing something nonrational or irrational does not commit rational preemptive suicide. A case of suicide might well satisfy our criteria except for the agent's last-minute perception of her act, which would suffice to rob that act of rationality. If, in the event, a suicidist were to judge her act of self-annihilation to be nonrational, she would not be taking her own life in the way required for rational preemptive suicide because either she would be right, in which case her suicide would not be rational because of failure to meet one or other criterion, or she would be confused about her reasoning and/or motives, in which case her act would not be a proper conclusion to her deliberation—regardless how sound the latter might be. Rational preemptive suicide is a fragile commodity, for it requires that the agent's well-reasoned deliberation be the real basis of its enactment, and that means that the agent cannot suddenly begin to vacillate about her motives or intentions at the moment of enactment. She must sustain her reasoning and resolution to the very end. Though ambivalence the agent may feel cannot be entirely eliminated, it must be minimal, as noted in Chapter 6, lest it disrupt the agent's resolve and her confidence in the reliability of her reasoning, deliberation, and assessment of her prospects. But this emphasis on the intentional should not be read as emphasis on the *private*. Not only must the agent satisfy external criteria in her deliberation and action, she requires the context provided by the practice of judging some cases of self-inflicted death as rational in order to be able to think of taking her own life and conducting her suicidal deliberation according to publicly acknowledged standards. Lacking an established practice, the suicidist could only conditionally—and courageously—take her own life as a demonstration of private conviction of the soundness of her own deliberation, and so of the possibility of rational preemptive suicide, and, perhaps, to provide a precedent. But the suicidist would then be faced with a vastly more difficult and daunting decision to make and sustain.

The constitutive role of the criteria for rational suicide does not only mean that they do not describe a misconceived independent archetype to which preemptive suicide conforms. It also means that there can be no appeal to an equally misconceived underlying objective rationality providing independent justification for a classificatory practice which could be engaged in or not without affecting its intrinsic nature. There can be no appeal to the autonomous correctness of the rationality criteria separate from their conformity to received standards, their general acceptance, and their practical productivity. As Richard Rorty tells us, "there is . . . no criterion that we have not created in the course of creating a practice, . . . no rigorous argumentation that is not obedience to our own conventions" (Rorty, 1982: xlii). The criteria for rational preemptive suicide enable some cases of suicide to be judged and described as preemptive and rational, and in that way provision of criteria delineating a viably construable phenomenon is introduction or reintroduction of a *practice*, not rediscovery of a forgotten Platonic archetype nor exercise of a reified objective rationality. Nonetheless, it should not be thought that we are left only with an arbitrary classificatory practice regarding suicide. To think so is the habitual reaction of those who, when denied apodictic certitude, ricochet to a hopeless relativism. The practice in question is based on well-established procedures. The ways we go about appraising something and drawing conclusions about it-our analytic methodologies and their attendant evaluatory and procedural criteria—were forged over millennia and are now very deeply entrenched because of their efficacy and progressive refinement. And those methodologies have solid bases in their conformity to our admittedly malleable, but really quite stable human nature, and the ways of thinking and judging that nature entails. They also have the pragmatic validation of a long and, at least recently, well-documented history (Prado, 1987). The proposed practice of judging some cases of suicide rational does not raise questions about the methodologies which the practice presupposes. It only introduces or reintroduces criteria to enable the application of those methodologies, which are at present thought *not* applicable, to the deliberation and assessment of self-inflicted death. To acknowledge that the criteria at issue are not grounded in Cartesian certainty nor capable of being autonomously correct is only to make them relative to human history, interests, and intellectual evolution. It is not to foolishly abandon the project of "grounding" the criteria on still-elusive foundations and to hastily settle for erratic consensus. There *are no* such foundations. In accepting the historical nature of the criteria, as well as of our methodologies, we are only admitting the chimerical nature of philosophical foundationalism. To see this as abandonment of anything is only to manifest a puzzling but apparently profound human distrust of the merely human. The criteria for rational preemptive suicide clearly assume certain standards of acceptability: consistency, common—if not universal—priorities in reasoning, values, and interests, and generally *specific betterness* in thought and action. But these standards do not of themselves pose an issue, nor do their assumption and use. The onus is on challengers to show alternatives preferable. However, this is not the place to counter quixotic attempts to articulate or defend ahistorical definitions of rationality or foundational accounts on the one hand, or hopelessly permissive relativist views on the other. I can close this section by reiterating that the rationality criteria are partly constitutive of the rationality of preemptive suicide in the sense that they themselves establish what is rational, preemptive, self-inflicted death by saying when that description is applicable. That is, the criteria are not only *tests* for something; they are determinants of that something. The criteria are neither derived articulations of objective standards for rational preemptive suicide, nor are they merely statements of relativistic personal or group preferences. Instead they say when we—using our established ways of assessing and validating reasoning and behavior—can and will accept a case of suicide as rational and preemptive. What is new here is the idea that our standard ways of assessing thought and action

do apply to a special sort of self-inflicted death, one not thought
rational for a long time. And this means that in the relevant cases
of suicide we will not look for *causes*, though we may certainly
look for reasons.

Competing Conceptions of Suicide

Contrasting rational preemptive suicide with causally explained suicide requires at least brief discussion of how suicide
is seen as or made amenable to causal explanation. Battin's
reminder that our culture largely conceives of suicide as
pathological—that is, as patho-psychologically caused—is not
just a point about popular views. As mentioned earlier, the
more theoretical levels of culture not only share that general
view, they provide the technical wherewithal for it. But it is only
after having clarified the nature of preemptive suicide that I can
say a little about prevalent competing conceptions of suicide. To
have begun with an inventory of those conceptions, and gone on
to discuss preemptive suicide in contrast to them, would have
been to assume the distinctness of the latter as a kind. And
given that its rationality is a *defining* characteristic of preemptive
suicide, to assume its distinctness would have been to effectively
presuppose the rationality at issue. I have discussed surcease and
anticipatory surcease suicide in addition to preemptive suicide,
and also alluded to self-sacrificial or altruistic suicide, as well
as to pathological, confused, and compelled suicide. But while
readily enough characterizable for the purpose of indentificatory
contrast, each of these sorts of suicide is open to different
theoretical conceptions.

Something must now be said about these, since it is theoretical conception that determines how each of the several sorts of
suicide admits of causal explanation. Depending on the theory
favored, causal explanation of suicide may range from causal
factors construed as influences of varying strength on the agent's
deliberation and action, to mechanistic construals of causal factors
which render deliberation and volition epiphenomenal or simply
illusory. Putting aside the causal but too ill-defined popular
conception of suicide, we can distinguish between two broad
groups of theoretical conceptions which support largely causal

accounts of suicide. The first group includes what I will call "holistic-theory" conceptions of suicide. In contrast to the specificity characteristic of conceptions in the second group, those in this first group tend to be broadly inclusive and offer homogeneous views of suicide. These conceptions resist internal differentiation of types of suicide and hence are more readily able to offer exhaustive causal explanations using a single set of principles. Each holistic-theoretical conception of suicide is a product of a different universalistic perspective which includes an account of self-inflicted death as a function of its general organizational and explanatory principles. In other words, suicide is not treated as a special problem, but as one of the phenomena that the general theory must cover in its broad understanding of human behavior. Holistic-theoretical conceptions of suicide compete most directly with rational preemptive suicide because none tolerate it as a special case, and assimilation of preemptive suicide to any causal account would strip it of the kind of rationality it must have. The holistic-theoretical conceptions which are of greatest importance in the present context are the two most widely accepted as satisfactorily explaining human behavior in general and suicide in particular. Both conceptions basically deny the possibility of the fully rational deliberation and enactment preemptive suicide requires. Both conform to and reinforce common expectations and are in fact the main sources of those expectations. The first of the two conceptions in question is the Durkheimian sociological conception of suicide, which focuses on the dynamics of the agent's relation to her society and hence on sociological motivation for elective death. The second is the Freudian psychological conception, which focuses on the agent's internal dynamics and hence on internal, mainly emotional motivation (DeSpelder, 1987: 407-12; Durkheim, 1912; Freud, 1915).

The main danger posed to rational preemptive suicide by the Durkheimian and Freudian conceptions—as well as other holistic-theoretical conceptions of suicide, such as a Marxist one—is the same: assimilation to a theoretical category in which its rationality is decisively circumscribed and so effectively denied or fatally qualified. If preemptive suicidal deliberation and self-inflicted death are explained in terms of Emile Durkheim's category

of "egoistic" suicide, wherein suicide is due to "excessive
individualism" (Durkheim, 1912: 174–232), the rationality of
that deliberation and action is undermined because subjugated
to social forces over which the agent has little or no control and
of which she is not fully aware (DeSpelder, 1987: 409). If suicidal
deliberation and self-inflicted death are explained in Freudian
terms as products of greatly stressful internal conflicts, they are
depicted as involving a definitively characteristic and overriding
ambivalence which undermines their rationality in a different but
equally conclusive way (Freud, 1915).

Generally, the rationality of preemptive suicide will be interpreted within a theoretical structure as only efficacious
means-to-ends thinking which serves essentially nonrational
and largely imposed values, goals, and motives. Therefore, the
criteria I have set out could not be satisfied. Even if Narveson's
requirement were met, and the theoretically conceived imposed
values, goals, and motives were shown to be themselves rational,
holistic-theoretical conception of the values, goals, and motives
precisely turns on their claimed actual roles not being accessible
to the agent because of their nature and level of operation and the
fact that their primary purpose is control, if not manipulation, of
the agent. The nonimpairment criterion would suffice to block
the rationality of preemptive suicide (theoretically conceived in
one of the ways in question) because it rules out false beliefs on
the part of the potential suicidist, and it is inherent to the kind
of holistic theory we are considering here to postulate one or
another kind of "false consciousness" in human reasoning and
perception.

The vulnerability of preemptive suicide to theoretical assimilation is a consequence of the need to thicken the applicable senses
of "rational" and "rationality" with certain abstract values, such
as consistency, as well as more specific ones, such as the potential
suicidist's perception of the fittingness of her death. As we saw
in considering the reasonableness or thick-rationality problems
with the general's suicide, we would not get very far in our
discussion of preemptive suicide with a bare, value-neutral
notion of rationality as simply maximal efficacy of means to
given ends. Reason or rationality so thinly conceived could
only be Hume's purely instrumental "handmaid" to values and

emotions, and when applied to preemptive suicide could only be used to assess the efficiency of the agent's actions. However, the moment we introduce values which determine ends—and which therefore drive, focus, and guide efficacious means-thinking or narrowly conceived rationality—we invite theoretical construal of the nature, origins, hierarchical ordering, and power of those values. And since we do not each generate our values out of nothing, it is legitimate enough to offer theories of where and how we get even our most basic values and how they move us and govern our behavior. It is always possible, then, to construe a suicidist's deliberation and action as prompted by socially or psychologically imposed values, and to reduce rational deliberation to rationalization. The reduction of the roles and importance of volition and reasoning is achieved through imposition of a structure within which the agent's intellect and will serve ends dictated by external factors. As was noted in connection with the quotation from Bullock's dictionary in Chapter 1, the "rational" in "rational suicide" then means only that suicidal action is consistent with the agent's or her group's possibly eccentric principles and logic, and that her suicide is not rational by external criteria. Suicide might be deemed "rational" according to heavily religious or political criteria which would not be widely accepted or acceptable. Abstract theoretical explanations of suicide generally objectify the agent's deliberations and actions in ways which usually mean that suicide is invariably rendered "rational" by agent or group standards, and as invariably is never rational by observer or theory standards. Unfortunately I do not know how to argue for a thick conception of rationality which would be somehow transtheoretical without claiming to be ahistorical. All I can do is point to how we do in fact manage to assess holistic-theoretical perspectives. Even if such assessment is always carried out from within another holistic-theoretical perspective, we do have principles and procedures that are either common to those perspectives or in some way overreach them. Regardless of philosophical relativism—and thanks largely to Donald Davidson—we are not in a hopeless conceptual-scheme relativism wherein holistic perspectives cannot be assessed and allow only acceptance or rejection (Davidson, 1973–74). But in any case, I do not think it necessary to argue for a grand, transtheoretical conception of rationality. The argumentative onus here is on those who offer all-inclusive theoretical frameworks to explain human behavior. The criteria and requirements which I have provided seem to me to describe a possible sort of suicide with respect to which it cannot be *simply* maintained that any instance of allegedly rational preemptive suicide is just an instance of social or psychological causes effecting more or less benighted self-inflicted death. In short, once criterially described, rational preemptive suicide stands until it is conclusively shown assimilable to some other sort.

The second group of competing conceptions of suicide can be dubbed "typal" because they are more narrowly defined kinds and, though theory-related, are considerably less theory-laden than those in the holistic-theory group. Each conception in the second group owes its specificity not to such details as the actual method of self-annihilation, but to being defined contextually in terms of the psychological, cultural, ethical, and/or physical conditions affecting deliberation about, experimentation with, and commission of, suicide (DeSpelder, 1987: 412–17). Examples are suicide where the agent takes her life because of psychotic delusions, or because of lack of viable options, as in cases of socially forced self-immolation by wives on the death of their husbands. Of these typal conceptions, surcease suicide, particularly in terminal illness, is the only one relevant to the discussion of the foregoing chapters, and then only as a counterpoint to our central interest in suicide committed prior to the onset of punishing conditions which force suicidal consideration and enactment. As for how typal conceptions generally relate to rational preemptive suicide, in most cases there should arise only classificatory questions regarding whether a given suicide is of one or another sort. What is important is that rational preemptive suicide be accepted as constituting one of these typal conceptions, as opposed to always being reducible to another. With respect to either the holistic-theory or more limited typal conceptions of suicide, then, the objective is to have rational preemptive suicide stand as a distinct kind of self-annihilation. Once the criteria and requirements for rational preemptive suicide are provided, the main task is to defend the cases they identify from assimilation to a competing sort. Clearly, though, doing so involves responding to specific reductive arguments, and so goes well beyond the scope of my present project. The serious and unavoidable problem posed by preemptive suicide for this project is that as the ultimate preventive act, it must be a paradigmatic case of rational action. But at the same time, since it is self-inflicted death apparently least adequately prompted and justified, it seems the most difficult to show to be rational. This problem neither requires nor is resolved by holistic-theoretical construals of suicide; it arises because preemptive suicide in advanced age is the forfeiture of life for somewhat elusive *envisaged* reasons. The trouble is that because of their nature those reasons seem too slender to support the enormity of the action contemplated and possibly taken.

Coherency Again

As just noted, the main obstacle to making out the rationality of preemptive suicide, and thereby establishing it as a unique sort of self-annihilation, is that because it is suicide deliberated and committed prior to serious pressures on the agent, it seems inadequately justified and so difficult to accept as a plausible object of rational deliberation and choice. Quite simply, if we fail to understand the justification for preemptive suicide, and so cannot comprehend how anyone could choose to commit it, we will think that no one *can* do so without confusion or compulsion. To acknowledge this possibility is not to retract the contention made in Chapter 7 that the issue of whether preferring to die can be coherent is adequately dealt with through attrition by satisfaction of the rationality criteria. Rather it is to acknowledge that the matter is even more complex than it first appeared. It is to admit that while a general skepticism about coherently preferred death can be dealt with, the practical reality may still elude us. What emerges when we consider theoretical alternatives to preemptive suicide, and see how preemptive suicide could be vulnerable to assimilation to one of those alternatives, is just how hard it is to make sense of preemptive suicide as a unique, knowing, deliberate, and rationally justified act.

Theoretical accounts do offer us effective and often conceptually satisfying ways of understanding why someone might take her own life, but they mostly do so by reducing the knowingness and deliberateness of the act. Against this, preemptive suicide, as I have described it, requires that we understand and appreciate wholly knowing and deliberate abandonment of life for the sake of avoiding what is only foreseen. It is no surprise that lingering doubts reassert themselves and we seem to be brought back to the basic question raised in Chapter 1, namely, whether preemptive suicide *can* be rational in the sense of whether it can be coherent to prefer to die.

The first thing to appreciate here is that satisfaction of the criteria for rational preemptive suicide does exhaust the content of the *philosophical* question about the coherency of preferring to die. To demand more than satisfaction of the criteria would be to misguidedly require abstract ways of incontrovertibly establishing the presence or absence of impossibly determinate and unchanging thoughts, assessments, values, and intentions in the minds of particular individuals during their suicidal deliberations and the moments of their deaths. It would be to want Cartesian certainty in an area where it is even more hopeless than in others. But a question does remain about whether an agent can coherently prefer annihilation for the certitude of avoiding something she only anticipates, and do so while she is still living an acceptable life. However, we have made a good deal of progress, because the question we now face is a significantly more limited and manageable one. Rather than being an open question about the rationality of suicide or the coherence of the preference for death, the question is now one about *relative evaluation*.

We are now able to pin down reservations about the coherency of preemptive suicide to the difficulty of understanding how it can make sense for an agent to willingly forfeit viable existence because she judges that what she only fears will happen outweighs months or even years of satisfactory and possibly rewarding life. Furthermore, it must be kept in mind that what the potential suicidist would die to avoid is something she does not *want* to bear, rather than something she will be *unable* to bear. Preemptive suicide therefore involves two highly problematic characteristics: first, the agent acts because of envisaged reasons—as opposed to less questionable actual suffering that may justify surcease suicide, or the expected suffering that may justify anticipatory surcease suicide. Second, the agent is only unwilling to endure personal diminishment, as opposed to knowing she will be unable to stand it. Nor are matters made easier if we grant that the satisfactoriness of the agent's life is increasingly precarious because of her age. So long as her life *is* satisfactory, we think life too valuable to relinquish on the basis of fear as opposed to actual or at least soundly anticipated torment. And this idea is intensified by our conviction that the horrors of what is feared may be overestimated by the agent. We have a decided proclivity toward a diffuse optimism when it comes to considering willful self-annihilation as an alternative to any but the most punishing situation. And the proclivity is not without basis.

Human beings are immensely adaptable. They seem able to bear much they could not earlier imagine enduring, and to achieve some satisfaction while doing so. A recent article on hospices aptly illustrates the central point: "A hospice is a place where . . . a pretty hairdo or a good shave . . . take on vital importance. The lesson one learns . . . is at once life's most basic and elusive: You live until you die" (Martin, 1989). This is the basis for the optimistic proclivity, and, in effect, the most serious single point against preemptive suicide. But the point should not be confused with the platitudinous idea that "while there's life there's hope" if that means hope for *betterment*. The thrust of the article was that people in hospices manage to find and make value in their lives after having accepted the reality and finality of their terminal conditions, and even though often in pain. The point is just that while one does live, it is possible to realize value. This is the force of the Beeman objection, discussed in Chapter 2, to the effect that reduced circumstances do not preclude a measure of fulfillment and gratification. How can it—literally—make sense, then, to willingly sacrifice even a little good time to avoid what is still problematic with respect to its actual occurrence, and which in any case may not be as bad as imagined? What all of this comes to is that, after all, perhaps only surcease suicide can be fully rational, and preemptive suicide must always be less than rational to just the extent that we cannot know the future with anything remotely approaching certainty.

A Necessary Compromise?

It may appear at this point that even the more limited coherence question must force the argument for rational preemptive suicide to take a different direction. Assuming a continuing concern to guard against personal diminishment, and an unwillingness to forgo the possibility of rational preemptive suicide altogether— through acceptance that only surcease suicide can be rational—a "compromise" position might be made out as follows: (Modified) preemptive suicide to avoid personal diminishment may be rational, despite being committed prior to surcease conditions, if properly deliberated when there is sound prognostication that an *existent* but still benign terminal condition will soon produce neurophysiological deterioration and consequent diminishment. The "neurophysiological deterioration" qualification is needed to rule out cases where the terminal condition normally ends in death not preceded by impairment or other malady-related diminution of intellectuality. This compromise basically assimilates preemptive suicide to anticipatory surcease suicide. But it can claim to preserve the essence of preemptive suicide in spite of requiring that suicide be deliberated and committed in the context of an actual terminal condition. It does so by relying on adequate medical evidence of eventual deterioration, as well as experience with the particular terminal disease, to time suicide in advance of even the earliest signs of diminishment. In this way a distinction is maintained between the revised preemptive suicide and anticipatory surcease suicide, by making the former appropriate in cases of anticipated mental diminishment and the latter appropriate in cases of painful physical deterioration. The proposed compromise is important because as a position it captures the "sensible" view that life should be surrendered only for adequately compelling reasons. And it does resolve the more limited coherency question by requiring that the agent face an actual terminal prognosis which provides real motivation for suicidal deliberation. Certainly many will feel that the proffered compromise version of preemptive suicide is all that is needed because preemptive suicide achieves nothing that cannot be achieved with flexibly construed anticipatory surcease suicide. The compromise position, then, is a repudiation of the need for the unique form of self-inflicted death defined by the provided criteria. And it is less an attempt to salvage preemptive suicide than to exhaust its possible applications by allowing wider temporal margins and more diffuse reasons in the justification of anticipatory surcease suicide. To counter the offered compromise I must show that it misses important aspects of preemptive suicide, and so fails to displace preemptive suicide as a unique kind of elective death.

Trying to assimilate preemptive to anticipatory surcease suicide would first require adjustment of the formulation and application of the nonimpairment criterion to allow an agent's *earlier* suicidal deliberation and decision to apply at a later time. This would be necessary to guard against the later timing of suicide resulting in enough deterioration to hamper adequate deliberation and judgment. That is, since suicide would follow diagnosis of a terminal condition likely to affect intellectuality, the possibility would exist that as the diagnosed condition progressed through even its earliest stages it might directly or indirectly impair the agent's reasoning. The agent would have to deliberate and decide about suicide immediately on being diagnosed as terminal and, if she opted for suicide, she would pick an opportune time for its enactment. To conform to the spirit of the compromise position, that time would be as late as possible but prior to indications of deterioration. Nonetheless, suicide would still have to be the agent's *own* act to prevent her death being euthanatic. That means a very fine balance would have to be struck. Suicide would have to be timed late enough that a reasonable maximum of life was enjoyed, since that is precisely the point of the proposed compromise, but not late enough to prevent the agent from taking her own life knowingly and deliberately—even if on the basis of earlier deliberation and decision. I think this "adjustment" of the nonimpairment criterion unworkable. The time-lapse between suicidal deliberation and enactment raises hopeless difficulties comparable to those noted by Judge Wachtler in connection with precomatose rejection of life-support. Moreover, the idea that an agent might be somewhat impaired in reasoning but still able to responsibly take her life seems unintelligible unless brief moments of clarity are deemed sufficient. But even if the nonimpairment criterion could be adjusted as necessary, that would take care only of impairment due to deterioration. It would leave untouched the distorting influence of the agent's *knowledge* of her terminal condition. If suicide is not deliberated until there is actual evidence of a terminal condition, the agent's awareness of the diagnosis could warp her deliberation and *not* through deteriorative impedance of reasoning. For instance, abhorrence of even an incipient terminal condition could subtly or drastically color the agent's appraisal of what she might still accomplish and so incline her too much toward suicide, thus jeopardizing the rationality of her decision through unbalanced evaluation rather than defective thought. Knowledge of her condition could play a role similar to that of depression in the cases Battin describes. On the other hand, an optimistic estimate of trouble-free time available could lull the agent into delaying suicide beyond a point when it could be done with full knowledge and deliberateness.

The importance of the agent's knowledge raises a second criterial difficulty for the compromise position. The temporal criterion for rationality would have to be radically changed or abandoned. The compromise position explicitly precludes preemptive suicide considered and committed "sufficiently prior to imminent or actual deterioration for suicide to be unforced forfeiture of life to avoid personal diminishment," since the point of the position is that there be actual grounds for suicide. It might be thought that the criterion could be satisfied by suicide committed when a terminal condition is known to exist but is still entirely innocuous—assuming that possible. However, the criterion does not support that reading. The fifth criterion expressly excludes the possibility of suicide being preemptive if considered and committed under negative conditions advanced enough—and this must include advancement sufficient for diagnosis—for knowledge of those conditions to influence deliberation. The nub of the difficulty is that the compromise position assumes the incipient deteriorative condition it postulates is a terminal one, even though still in its earliest and most benign stages. This means that in light of the relevant diagnosis, the agent really has only two options: to accept the likely effects of her condition and live out her term, or to end her life prior to suffering those effects. The agent's choice is no longer an unforced one. She has lost the opportunity of making her suicide preemptive in the sense that her self-inflicted death be a value-prompted self-defining act and fitting end to her life. Knowledge of her condition makes her primary reason for suicide avoidance of the prognosticated deterioration. Even if well in advance of actual suffering, the "escape" nature of the agent's elective death is ensured by her knowledge of what she faces. The compromise position actually turns on avoidance of suffering becoming the dominant objective of suicide, which raises a related problem having to do with the motivation for preemptive suicide. Though there certainly may be early diagnoses of various deteriorative terminal conditions, it is much more problematic whether there can be early diagnosis of *diminishment*. Personal diminishment of the sort preemptive suicide guards against is not as reliably tied to specific neurophysiological and organic conditions as we might like—or as it may eventually be. The role of the agent's values and perceptions is crucial with respect to the assessment of diminishment, and so with respect to preemptive suicide. The role those values and perceptions play cannot be played by knowledge of a negative medical prognosis. For one thing, knowledge that she has a terminal condition, which can be counted on to shorten her life very considerably, might make suicide because of feared diminishment pointless in the agent's view. She may be willing to bear diminishment of short duration for the sake of not causing her family greater distress. These motivational considerations show that preemptive suicide is very different from the compromise position's extended version of anticipatory surcease suicide.

A more general problem with the compromise position is the underlying assumption that the value of what preemptive suicide achieves for an agent is automatically outweighed by whatever fulfillment or gratification may still be forthcoming in the last years of her life and even after terminal diagnosis. This assumption is what I have been contending against all along: the idea that continued life, under all but the very worst circumstances, is categorically the highest value and priority.

The assumption is a rejection of Seneca's point that sufficiently advanced age itself warrants preemptive suicide, both because of the growing likelihood of harrowing deterioration and because of what he saw as inherent limitations to the length of time a human being can live rewardingly. No argument is offered to support the implicit contention that we should simply live as long as we possibly can short of enduring horrendous distress. Worse still, a too-rosy, and certainly overly sentimental picture is painted of how life is conducted toward its close and even when a terminal condition has begun to have serious effects. Individuals, such as those in hospices, are pictured as heroically coping with their terminal conditions and squeezing the last drops of satisfaction from their lives. They are offered as shining examples of people living relatively rewarding lives in spite of their circumstances. However, at present, people in terminal conditions in or out of hospices usually have no choice but to make the best of their situations precisely because our culture does not provide them with a suicidal option. And their courage and resolve may be otiose and ill-conceived when compared with what they are forced to endure, since whatever value they may achieve is precisely achieved in very negative circumstances which likely outweigh that value. These people cannot be used as edifying examples, for the implication of so using them is that they are enduring their distress *by choice*, and for the sake of the value they occasionally attain. The reality is that they have no choice but to endure their situation and that the value gained is rare and often only a function of greatly reduced expectations. It is certainly doubtful that it even approaches adequate compensation for the circumstances from which it is wrested.

Perhaps the most serious problem with the compromise position is that it ignores what I argued in responding to the Beeman objection, namely, that the crux of the matter is *what the agent is willing to bear*. Two key points emerged in the earlier discussion: first, the question of the acceptability of age-related changes must be treated in terms of what particular individuals are willing to accept, not in terms of what is in some broad third-party sense deemed acceptable. The latter sort of judgment may be of great importance to an individual assessing her own situation, but it cannot be taken as providing a standard capable of precluding preemptive suicidal decisions. The second key point is that the changes age brings cannot be thought of as limited; it is not as if an aging individual suffers only degeneration of numerous but fairly delineated capacities. The central point is that it is *the person herself* that changes with age. If a stroke partially paralyzes an agent, or leaves her amnesiac in certain areas, it is possible that with time and therapy, the paralysis or amnesia can be overcome. Other muscles and/or parts of the brain may be trained to work in ways functionally similar to those affected by the stroke. But the changes that prompt preemptive suicide are not of this kind. They are not limited to a set of muscles or even parts of the brain or central nervous system that are addressable in some therapeutic way. The tragedy of the changes is that they are global. They affect the person herself in a holistic way, rather than handicapping or even crippling her in only some respects. The monstrosity of the diminishment occasioning preemptive suicide is that the individual suffering that diminishment is made into a lesser being, and one almost certainly unaware of the changes that have occurred except in the vaguest and most sporadic ways. The compromise position effectively disallows advanced age as *itself* grounds for preemptive suicide by requiring specific reasons over and above an agent's age for her to take her own life. This is to conceive of advanced age as a neutral condition only characterized by contingent maladies; it is to conceive of the human mind and body as not *themselves* deteriorated by time but as only afflicted with specific ills. The compromise position, then, precludes the agent's suicide as enactment of her *unwillingness to age beyond a certain point* in order not to become lessened.

The substance of the compromise view is that suicide would be not only preemptive, but *paradigmatically* so if considered and committed when there is already acute pressure on the agent in the form of a terminal prognosis of one or another sort. In effect, then, what the compromise view does is make central the cases which—following the conception I have been sketching—fall into a grey area between anticipatory surcease and preemptive suicide. And those cases which are central in my conception would become the marginal ones—not with respect to their preemptiveness, but with respect to their rationality. In accepting the compromise position, we would concede the common view that suicide can only be rational, or at least *fully* rational, when considered and committed in the face of disastrous circumstances. We would further concede that even greatly advanced age cannot itself count as a disastrous circumstance unless characterized by specific, diagnosable afflictions. The proposal does have a measure of plausibility, but mainly because it appeals to our feeling that there is no need to anticipate disaster and every reason to live as much of life as possible. But while the compromise position may itself constitute a viable enough stance with respect to elective death, it is not compelling enough to displace preemptive suicide as I have described it.

One apparently powerful point that might still be made in support of the compromise position, and against my emphasis on the agent's unwillingness to bear deteriorative changes, is that her readiness to commit preemptive suicide must be restricted by her obligations. The claim is that even a very elderly individual has responsibilities to her family, friends, and society at large, which preclude suicide except in contexts of terminal prognoses. I distrust this contention because I think it arises largely from the assumption that no one, whether elderly or otherwise, really has the right to dispose of her life. The objection has religious and social implications much more important than any ethical point it may contain, so it is likelier to represent efforts to manipulate the agent than to raise concerns about moral limits on her suicidal choice. It is true that an elderly individual may be a source of strength for someone, perhaps even for many people. But all this means is that the potential preemptive suicidist has one more factor to consider in her deliberation. It does not mean that preemptive suicide is just precluded by the very existence of certain responsibilities. We cannot allow dependencies to tyrannize an individual who likely would pay a considerably higher price to remain alive than the dependent persons would pay to cope alone. The case of a long-married couple may be an exception. Certainly suicide by one can be assumed, on the basis of what we see happening around us, to at least hasten the other's death. But again, this is a factor to be considered, not an absolute bar. While responsibilities of the sort in question must be considered and given due weight, we must agree with Hume that a man "who retires from life does no harm to society; He only ceases to do good; which, if it is an injury, is of the lowest kind" (Hume, 1963b: 109).

Conclusion

In spite of all that I have said it remains true that an elderly person cannot have certain knowledge of her future, can never be certain that preemptive suicide does *not* harm her more than staying alive. After all, what prompts her readiness to commit preemptive suicide is only fear that lessening changes in herself *might* eventuate, and that they *might* be wholly unacceptable. And so long as this is the case, it is also true that actually preferring to die for less than surcease reasons will be a difficult thing to achieve and must always appear implausible to others. But as I put it in Chapter 2, any one of us may come to judge that survival to an advanced age has seriously jeopardized our continued survival as the persons we are and value being, threatening to diminish us in ways we are unwilling to risk for the sake of a few more years of life. And surely so long as our biological nature remains what it is this judgment must be rational in the value- and interest-enhanced thick sense.

Age itself does count as a reason for ending one's life. But it will be evident from what has been said that preemptive suicide cannot be shown to be justified by feared diminishment if that means feared diminishment must override interest in continued life in the same way that actual suffering does. And we cannot have easy recourse to the idea that the fear of diminishment might be so great that it comes to constitute a surcease condition itself. That move works well enough as a justificatory one, but what it yields is not preemptive suicide in my sense, only another version of surcease suicide. Like the general's, the reflective aging individual's preemptive suicide is motivated by her *values*. Though she fears diminishment, she does not fear it as a candidate for anticipatory surcease suicide dreads inevitable torment or a candidate for surcease suicide seeks escape from agony. Nor is her preemptive suicide prompted by what so many think of when diminishment is discussed, namely, a horrific spectator's view of herself demeaned.

Preemptive suicide is not a function of *vanity*. The reflective aging individual moved to consider and possibly commit preemptive suicide is not consumed by terror of diminishment. That state is not compatible with a coolly rational assessment of one's prospects and a preemptive suicidal decision. The potential preemptive suicidist does not want to be lessened; she understands that her age makes it likely that she soon will be lessened or that she has already begun to be lessened. And she understands that the only alternative open to her is to end her life. She also understands that in ending her life at the right time, she appropriates an inevitable event which would otherwise occur as a mere effect, and thus adds value to her life by making her death the final assertion of her will and values. In this way she makes her death the last act in her self-definition and self-creation; she finishes the life-project of defining herself. The trouble is that the intellectual character of our culture is post-Kantian; we believe that rational justification is always a matter of subsuming individual actions under general principles. And given now-operant principles, there is great resistance to the idea that suicide as assertion of individual will and values can be generally accepted as justifiable. That seems to open the door to suicide committed at will, which is a too "subjectivist" and frightening idea to many.

Even if some philosophers and other professionals believe that suicide in advanced enough age can be and probably mostly is rational, our culture still sees suicide as cowardly, driven, pathological, and *wrong*—not just in an ethical sense but as somehow contrary to nature. Some of my colleagues scoff at this, as if the general view does not matter. It is like when they speak of our culture as "secular," as if a staggering majority did not still believe in God and the "televangelists" lacked an audience. Whatever may be the case in the academy, the legal, social, and commonly moral reality is that suicide still calls for vindication of the agent's act by general principles, and at present those principles facilitate justification only when the agent faces some horrendous circumstance. What we must do is abandon the Kantian perspective and adopt the Freudian. As Rorty puts it, Kantian rationality "centers around . . . bring[ing] particular actions under general principles . . . Freud suggests that we need to return to the particular" (Rorty, 1989: 33). We must at least see that satisfaction of the criteria for rational preemptive suicide is a complex matter of meeting certain general principles and then adding the crucial particulars: specifically, the reflective aging individual's assessment of her situation and her perception of her death as fitting. Preemptive suicide will then be recognized as fully justifiable. What emerges is that the decisive factor in what we might describe as the "deep acceptability" of preemptive suicide is perception of the fittingness of self-inflicted death. That perception is not only the necessary enhancement which turns preemptive suicide into a Jamesian live option, it is also the factor which compensates for preemptive suicide's justificatory shortfall when compared with anticipatory surcease and surcease suicide. The perception in question is, of course, the agent's. What I have tried to do in this book is contribute to *cultural* perception of that fittingness.

BIBLIOGRAPHY

Alvarez. Al. 1987. *The Savage God*. New York: Penguin Books.

Armstrong, David M. 1968. *A Materialist Theory of the Mind*. Oxford: Routledge and Kegan Paul.

Baechler, Jean. 1975. *Suicides*. Trans. Barry Cooper. New York: Basic Books.

Baltes, Paul, and K. W. Schaie. 1974. "Aging and I.Q.: The Myth of the Twilight Years." *Psychology Today* 7: 35–38, 40.

Battin, Margaret Pabst. 1987. "Choosing the Time to Die: The Ethics and Economics of Suicide in Old Age." In Stuart Spicker, Stanley Ingman, and Ian Lawson (eds.), *Ethical Dimensions of Geriatric Care: Value Conflicts for the 21st Century*. Dordrecht: Reidel.

————. 1982. "The Concept of Rational Suicide." *Ethical Issues in Suicide*. Englewood Cliffs: Prentice–Hall. Reprinted in Edwin S. Shneidman (ed.). 1984. *Death: Current Perspectives*. Palo Alto: Mayfield Publishing, pp. 297–320.

Bernstein, Richard. 1983. *Beyond Objectivism and Relativism*. Philadelphia: University of Pennsylvania Press.

Birren, James E. 1968a. "Aging: Psychological Aspects." In David Sill (ed.). 1968. *The International Encyclopedia of the Social Sciences*. Vol. 1. New York: Macmillan.

————. 1968b. "Psychological Aspects of Aging: Intellectual Functioning." *Gerontologist* 8: 16–19.

Birren, James E., and K. Warner Schaie (eds.). 1977. *Handbook of the Psychology of Aging*. New York: Van Nostrand.

Blythe, Ronald. 1979. *The View in Winter*. New York: Harcourt Brace Jovanovich.

Bond, E. J. 1988. " 'Good' and 'Good for': A Reply to Hurka." *Mind* 97: 279–80.

Boswell, James. 1947. "An Account of My Last Interview with David Hume, Esq." (1777). Reprinted as Appendix A in Norman Kemp Smith, *Hume's Dialogues Concerning Natural Religion*, 2d. ed. London: Thomas Nelson and Sons.

Botwinick, Jack. 1967. *Cognitive Processes in Maturity and Old Age*. New York: Springer.

Brandt, R. B. 1975. "The Morality and Rationality of Suicide." In Seymour Perlin (ed.), *A Handbook for the Study of Suicide*. Oxford: Oxford University Press, pp. 61–75.

Brentano, Franz. 1961. "The Distinction between Mental and Physical Phenomena." Trans. D. B. Terrell. In R. M. Chisholm (ed.), *Realism and the Background of Phenomenology*. Glencoe: The Free Press, pp. 39–61. (Trans. of Vol. I, Ch. 1, of Brentano's 1874 *Psychologie vom empirischen Standpunkt*.)

Bromley, D. B. 1974. *The Psychology of Human Aging*. London: Penguin.

Bullock, A., O. Stallybrass, and S. Trombley (eds.). 1988. *The Fontana Dictionary of Modern Thought*. London: Fontana.

Camus, Albert. 1955. *The Myth of Sisyphus and Other Essays*. Trans. J. O'Brien. New York: Knopf.

Choron, Jacques. 1972. *Suicide*. New York: Scribner's Sons.

Cowley, Malcolm. 1982. *The View from Eighty*. London: Penguin.

Currents. 1988. "Survivors." WNET–TV, Boston (Channel 13, New York), broadcast September 25, 1988.

Davidson, Donald. 1973–74. "On the Very Idea of a Conceptual Scheme." *Proceedings of the American Philosophical Association*. 17: 5–20.

Denny, N. W. 1979. "Problem Solving in Later Adulthood." In P. Baltes, and O. G. Brimm (eds.), *Life Span Development and Behavior*, Vol 2. New York: Academic Press, pp. 37–66.

DeSpelder, Lynne, and Albert Strickland. 1987. "Suicide." Chapter 13, *The Last Dance: Encountering Death and Dying*. Palo Alto: Mayfield Publishing Co.

Donnelly, John. 1978. "Suicide and Rationality." In *Language, Metaphysics, and Death*. New York: Fordham University Press, pp. 88–105.

Durkheim, Emile. 1912. *Le Suicide*. Paris: Librairie Félix Alcan. Trans. John Spaulding and George Simpson. 1966. *Suicide: A Study in Sociology*. New York: Free Press.

Edwards, Paul (ed.). 1967. *The Encyclopedia of Philosophy*, Vol. 4. New York: Macmillan and The Free Press.

Farber, Leslie H. 1969. "The Phenomenology of Suicide." In E. Shneidman, (ed.), *On the Nature of Suicide*. San Francisco: Jossey–Bass, pp. 109–110.

Feinberg, Joel. 1984. *Harm to Others*. Vol. 1 of *The Moral Limits of the Criminal Law*. New York: Oxford University Press.

Freud, Sigmund. 1915. "Our Attitude towards Death." Chapter 2, *Thoughts for the Times on War and Death*. *The Standard Edition of the Complete Works of Sigmund Freud*. London: Hogarth Press. Quoted in Battin, 1982: 318, n3.

Harman, Gilbert. 1986. *Change in View: Principles of Reasoning*. Cambridge: MIT Press.

Henig, Robin M. 1981. *The Myth of Senility: Misconceptions about the Brain and Aging*. New York: Doubleday.

Hinton, John. 1967. *Dying*. New York: Penguin.

Hoffmeister, F., and C. Muller (eds.). 1979. *Brain Function in Old Age: Evaluation of Change and Disorder*. New York: Springer.

Hook, Sidney. 1988. "The Uses of Death." *The New York Review* 25(7): 22–25.

Hume, David. 1963a. "My Own Life." (1776). In *Essays: Moral, Political and Literary*. Oxford: Oxford University Press.

———. 1963b. "On Suicide." (1777). In *Essays: Moral, Political and Literary*. Oxford: Oxford University Press. Same as "Essay on Suicide," quoted by Battin. See Hume, 1826. Essay was written in 1776, as given by Battin, but was first published in 1777.

———. 1826. "Essay on Suicide." (1776). In *The Philosophic Works of David Hume*. Edinburgh: Black and Tait. Quoted in Battin, 1982: 312.

James, William. 1956. *The Will to Believe and Other Essays in Philosophy*. New York: Dover.

Jarvik, Lissy. 1979. *Psychological Symptoms and Cognitive Loss in the Elderly*. New York: Halsted.

Kallimachos. 1956. "Plato's Elysium." (305 B.C.). Trans. Dudley Fitts, *Poems from the Greek Anthology*. New York: New Directions, p. 137.

Kastenbaum, Robert. 1967. "Suicide as the Preferred Way of Death." In E. Shneidman (ed). 1976. *Suicidology: Contemporary Developments*. New York: Grune and Stratton.

———. 1964. *New Thoughts on Old Age*. New York: Springer.

Keats, John. 1955. *Ode to a Nightingale*. (1820). Quoted lines reprinted in *The Oxford Dictionary of Quotations*, 2d ed. London: Oxford University Press, p. 287.

Kushner, Howard. 1989. *Self-Destruction in the Promised Land*. New Brunswick: Rutgers University Press.

Lapp, Danielle C. 1987. *Don't Forget*. New York: McGraw–Hill.
Laurence, Margaret. 1964. *The Stone Angel*. Toronto: McClelland and Stewart.
Levin, Jack, and William Levin. 1980. *Ageism: Prejudice and Discrimination against the Elderly*. Belmont: Wadsworth.
MacIntyre, Alisdair. 1981. *After Virtue*. Notre Dame: University of Notre Dame Press.
———. 1977. "Epistemological Crises, Dramatic Narrative and the Philosophy of Science." *The Monist* 60(4): 453–72.
Martin, Douglas. 1989. "Creating Beauty Out of Suffering as Life Fades." *The New York Times*, Feb. 18, 1989, p. 31.
Martin, R. M. 1980. "Suicide and Self-sacrifice." In M. P. Battin, and D. J. Mayo (eds), *Suicide: The Philosophical Issues*. New York: St. Martin's.
McIntosh, John L., and Nancy J. Osgood. 1986. *Suicide and the Elderly*. Westport: Greenwood Press.
McKee, Patrick. 1988. "The Aging Mind: View from Philosophy and Psychology." *The Gerontologist* 28(1): 132–33.
Motto, Jerome. 1972. "The Right to Suicide: A Psychiatrist's View," *Life-Threatening Behavior* 2(3): 183–88. New York: Behavioral Publications.
Narveson, Jan. 1986. "Moral Philosophy and Suicide." *Canadian Journal of Psychiatry* 31: 104–7
Nietzsche, Friedrich. 1967. *Will to Power*. Walter Kaufmann (ed.). New York: Random House.
———. 1954. *Thus Spake Zarathustra*. (Part One, 1883). In Walter Kaufmann (ed.), *The Portable Nietzsche*. New York: Viking Press.
Oates, Joyce Carol. 1980. "The Art of Suicide." In M. P. Battin and D. J. Mayo (eds.). 1980. *Suicide: Philosophical Issues*. New York: St. Martin's Press, pp. 161–68.
Palmore, Erdman. 1971. "Attitudes Toward Aging as Shown by Humor." *Gerontologist* 11: 181–86.
Parfit, Derek. 1971. "Personal Identity." *The Philosophical Review*. 80: 3–27.
Perlin, Seymour. 1975. *Handbook for the Study of Suicide*. Oxford: Oxford University Press.
Prado, C. G. 1988. "Aging and Narrative." In James Thorton and Earl Winkler (eds.), *Ethics and Aging*, pp. 215–22.
———. 1987. *The Limits of Pragmatism*. Atlantic Highlands: Humanities Press.
———. 1986. *Rethinking How We Age: A New View of the Aging Mind*. Westport: Greenwood Press.

———. 1985. "Reference and the Composite Self." *International Studies in Philosophy*, 17: 25–33.

———. 1983. "Ageing and Narrative." *International Journal of Applied Philosophy*. 1(3): 1–13.

Ramberg, Bjorn. 1989. *Donald Davidson's Philosophy of Language: An Introduction*. Oxford: Basil Blackwell.

Robinson, Paul. 1984. *Criminal Law Defenses*. St. Paul: West Publishing Co.

Rorty, Richard. 1989. *Contingency, Irony, and Solidarity*. Cambridge: Cambridge University Press.

———. 1986. "The Contingency of Selfhood." *London Review of Books*, May 8, 1986.

———. 1982. *The Consequences of Pragmatism*. Minneapolis: University of Minnesota Press.

Russell, Bertrand, and Alfred North Whitehead. 1910–13. *Principia Mathematica*. Cambridge: Cambridge University Press.

Salmon, Phillida. 1985. *Living in Time*. London: J. M. Dent and Sons.

Scanlon, T. M. 1975. "Preference and Urgency." *The Journal of Philosophy*. 72: 655–69.

Seneca. 1969. *Letters from a Stoic*. Letter 77. Trans. Robin Campbell. Baltimore: Penguin Books.

Shakespeare, William. 1953. *Measure for Measure*. Quoted in *The Oxford Dictionary of Quotations*, 2d ed. Oxford: Oxford University Press, p. 462.

Shipp, E. R. 1988. "New York's Highest Court Rejects Family's Plea in Right-to-Die Case" (and transcript excerpts) and "Many Courts Have Upheld Right to Die. "*The New York Times*, Oct. 15, 1988, pp. 1, 36.

Shneidman, E., and N. Farberow. 1957. "The Logic of Suicide." In *Clues to Suicide*. New York: McGraw–Hill.

Siegler, Ilene. 1976. "Aging I.Q.s." *Human Behavior* 5: 55.

Skinner, B. F., and M. E. Vaughan (eds.). 1983. *Enjoy Old Age*. New York: W. W. Norton.

Thorton, James, and Earl Winkler (eds.). 1988. *Ethics and Aging*. Vancouver: University of British Columbia Press.

Tierney, John. 1982. "The Aging Body." *Esquire*. May 1982, pp. 45–57. (Though published in a popular magazine, this article is very concise and illuminating and clearly well-researched.)

Tolchin, Martin. 1989. "When Long Life Is Too Much: Suicide Rises Among [the] Elderly." *The New York Times*, July 19, 1989, pp. 1, 10.

Wass, Hannalore, Felix Berardo, and Robert Neimeyer (eds.). 1987. *Dying: Facing the Facts*, 2d ed. New York: Hemisphere.

Williams, Bernard. 1973. "Imagination and the Self." In *Problems of the Self*. Cambridge: Cambridge University Press.

Williams, Gareth. 1986b, "Lay Beliefs about the Causes of Rheumatoid Arthritis: Their Implications for Rehabilitation." *International Rehabilitation Medicine* 8: 65–68.

———. 1984. "The Genesis of Chronic Illness: Narrative Reconstruction." *Sociology of Health and Illness* 6(2): 175–200.

Williams, Gareth, and Philip H. Wood. 1986a. "Common-sense Beliefs about Illness: A Mediating Role for the Doctor." *The Lancet*, Dec. 20/27.

INDEX

About the Author

C. G. PRADO is Professor of Philosophy at Queen's University, Kingston, Canada. He is the author of several articles and a book on the subject of philosophy and aging, as well as numerous articles and three books on other philosophical topics.

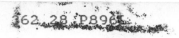

DATE DUE

SE 22 '91			
FE 07 '92			
JY 17 '92			
MR 23 '93			
DEC 27 '97			
5/14/98			